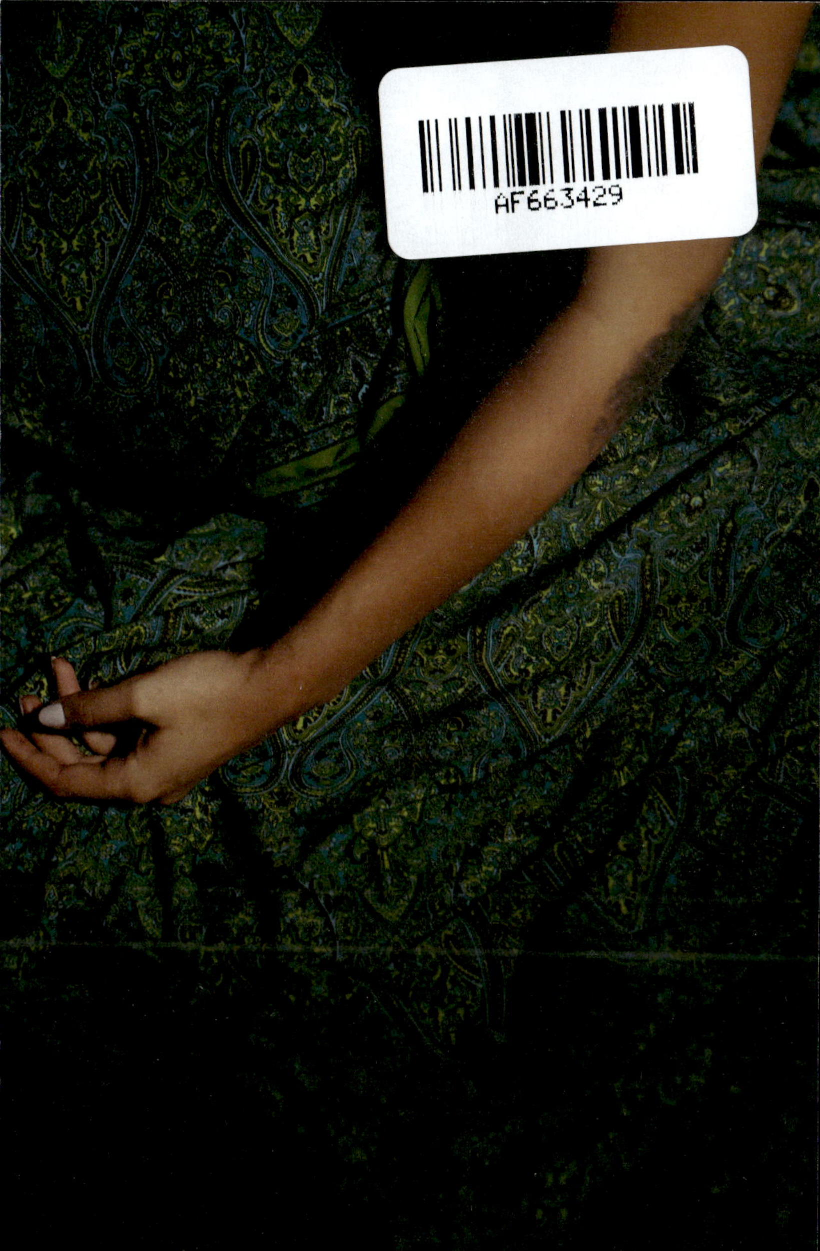

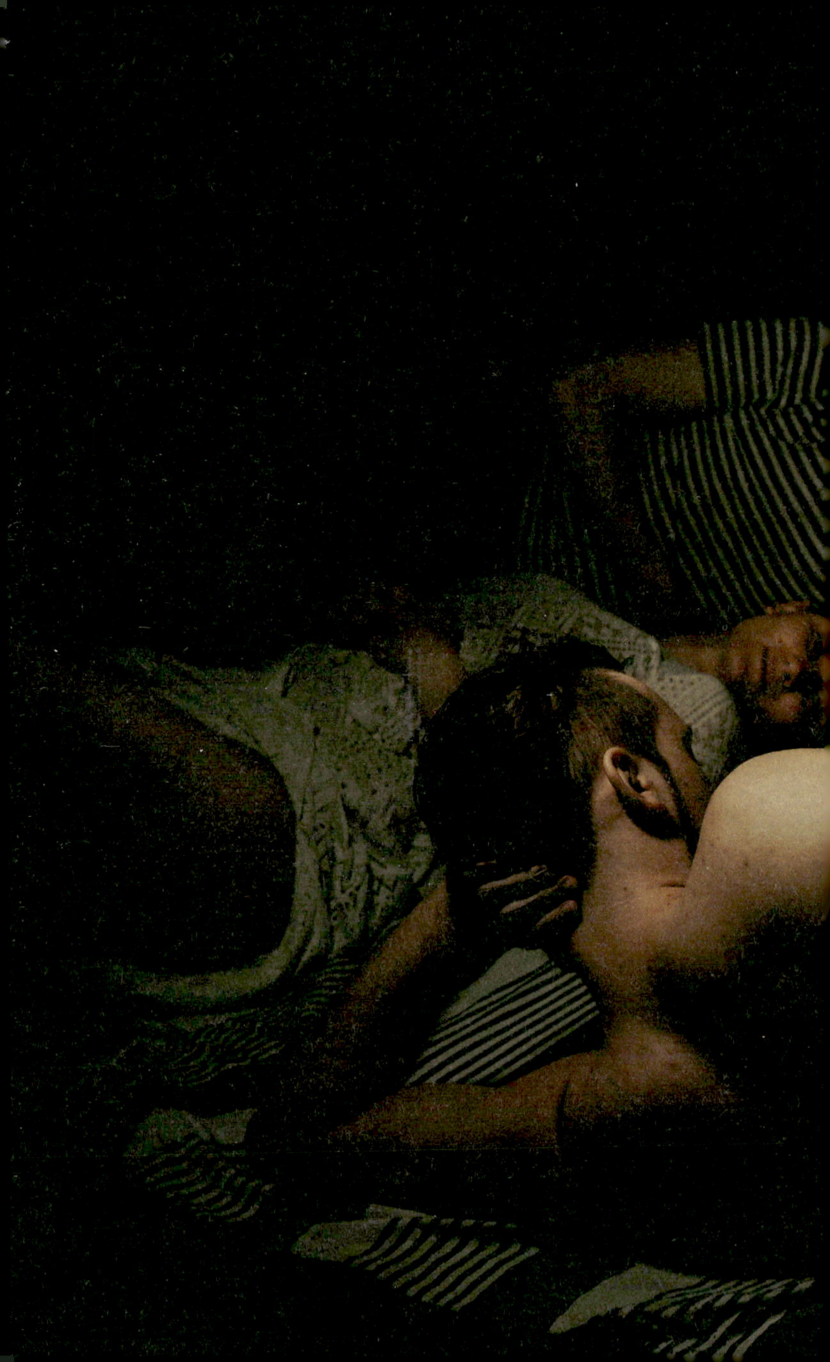

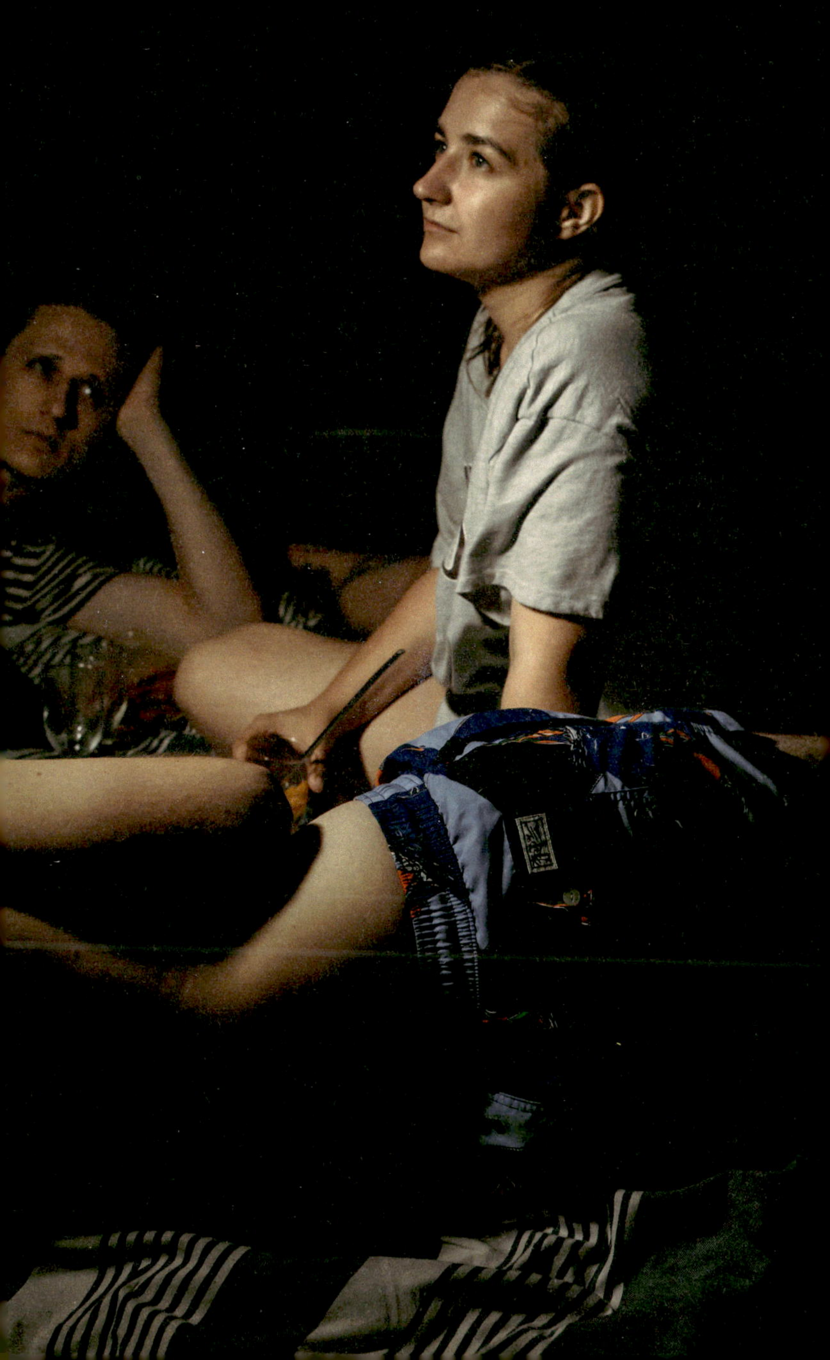

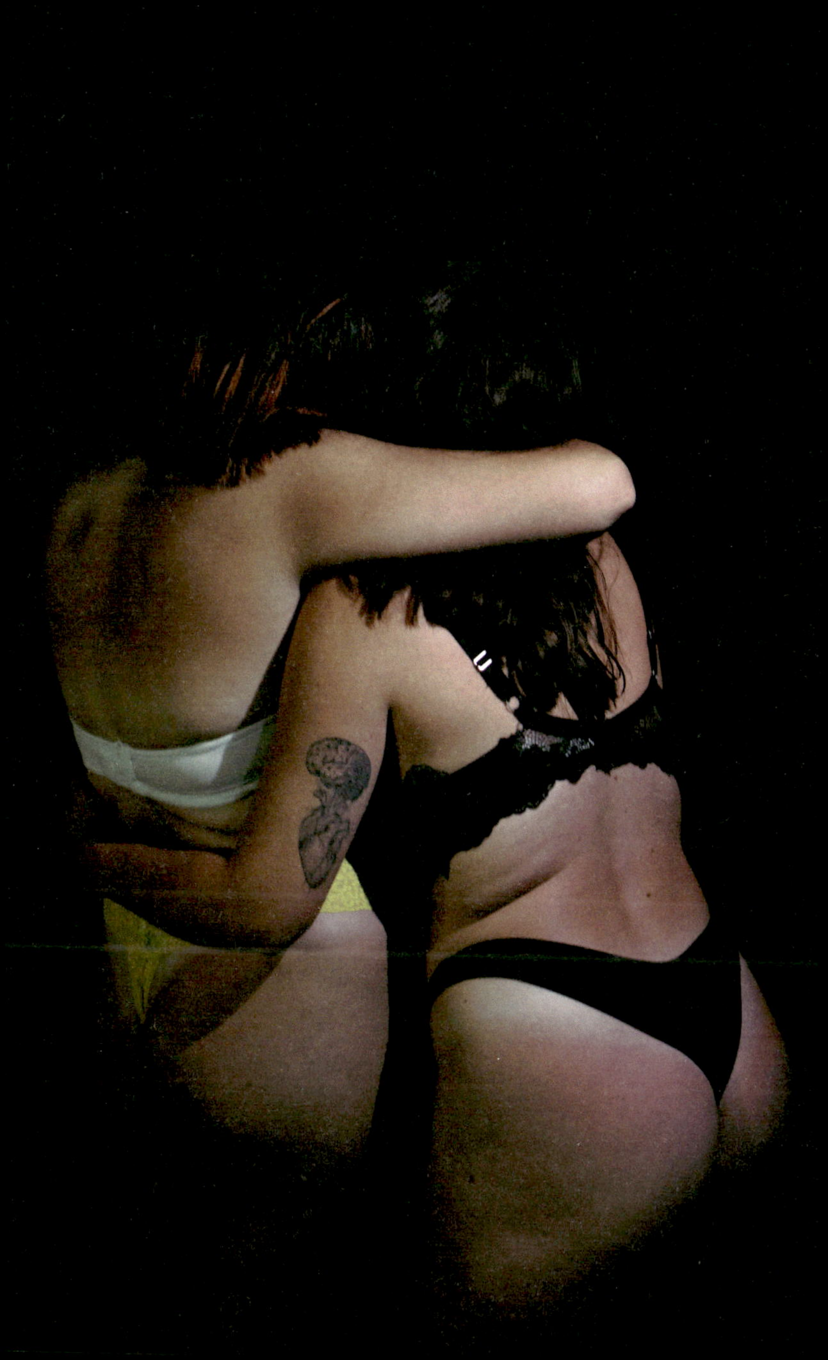

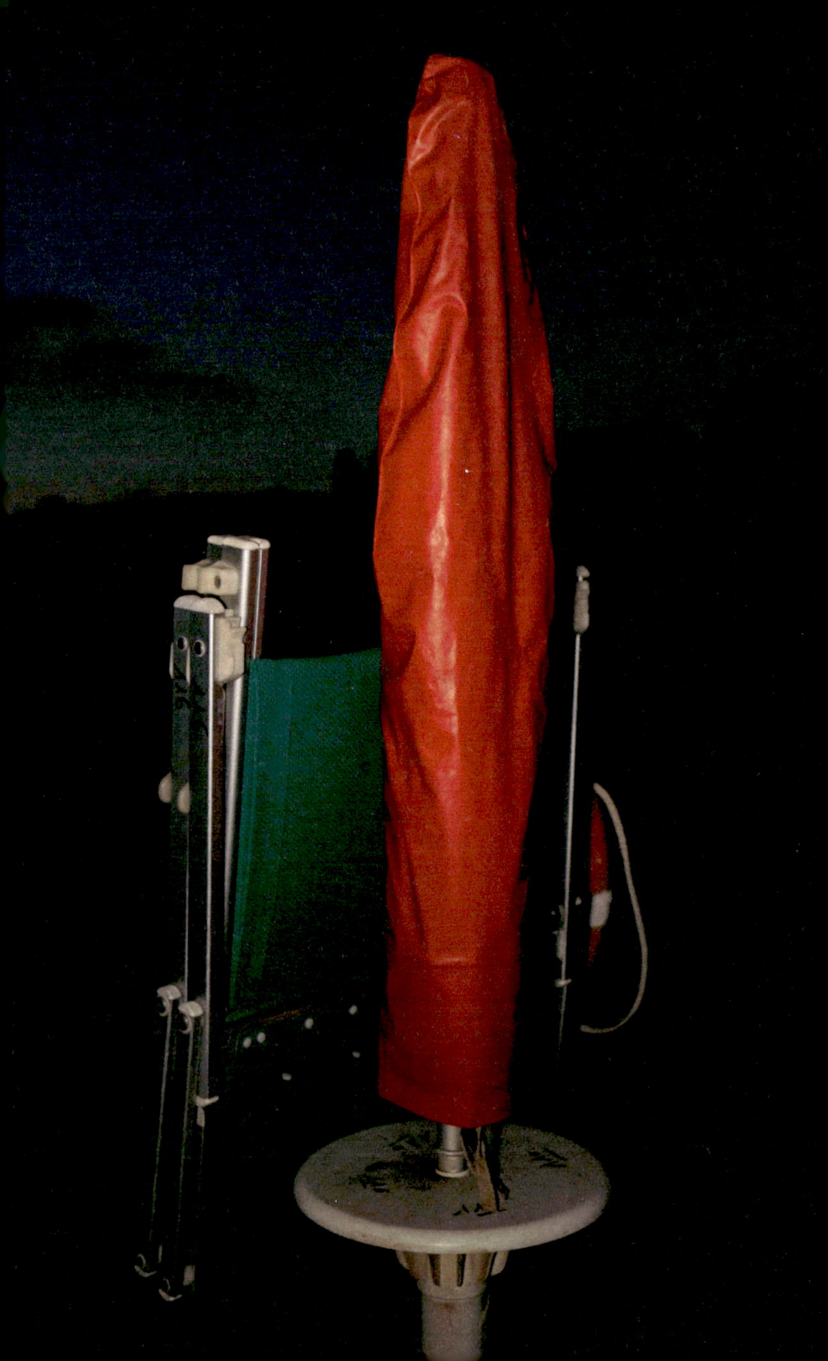

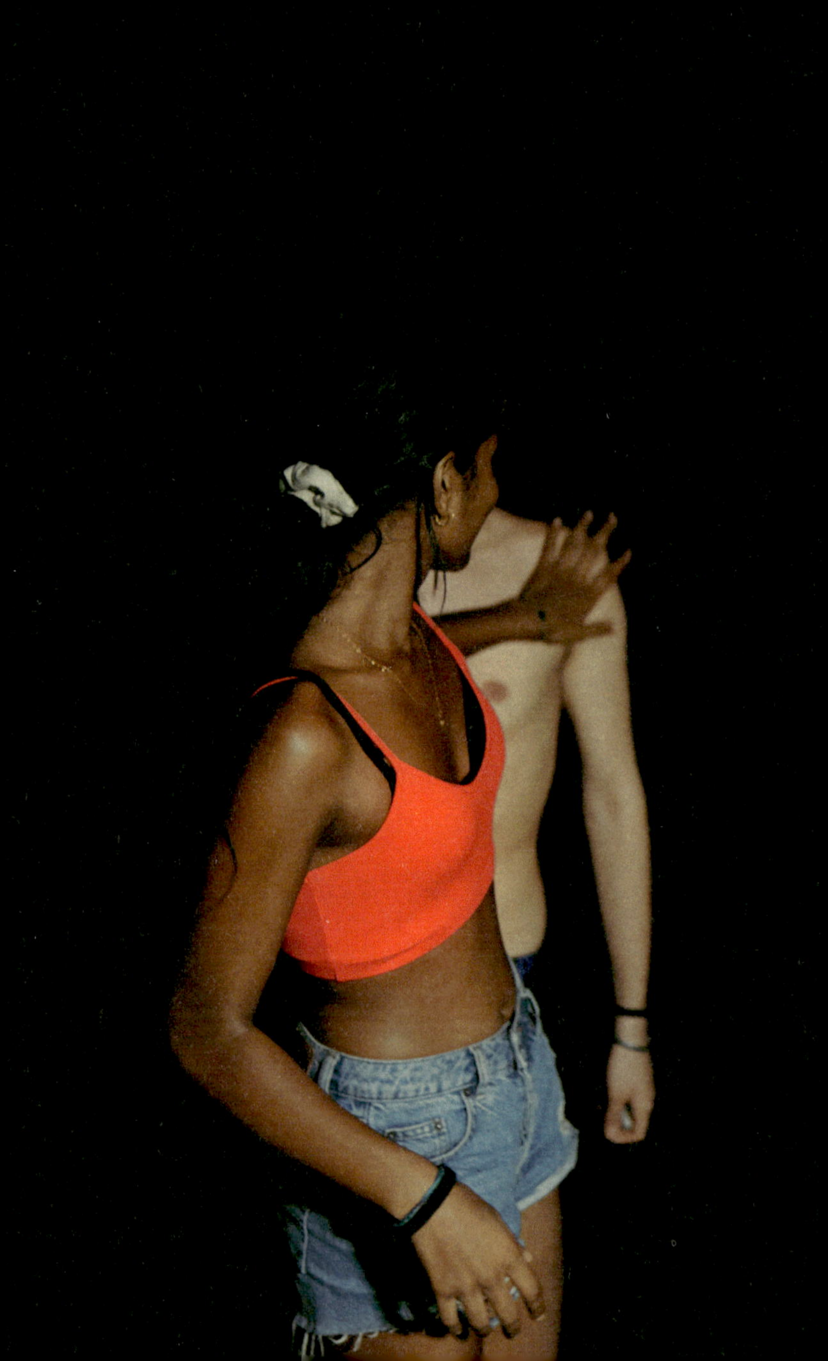

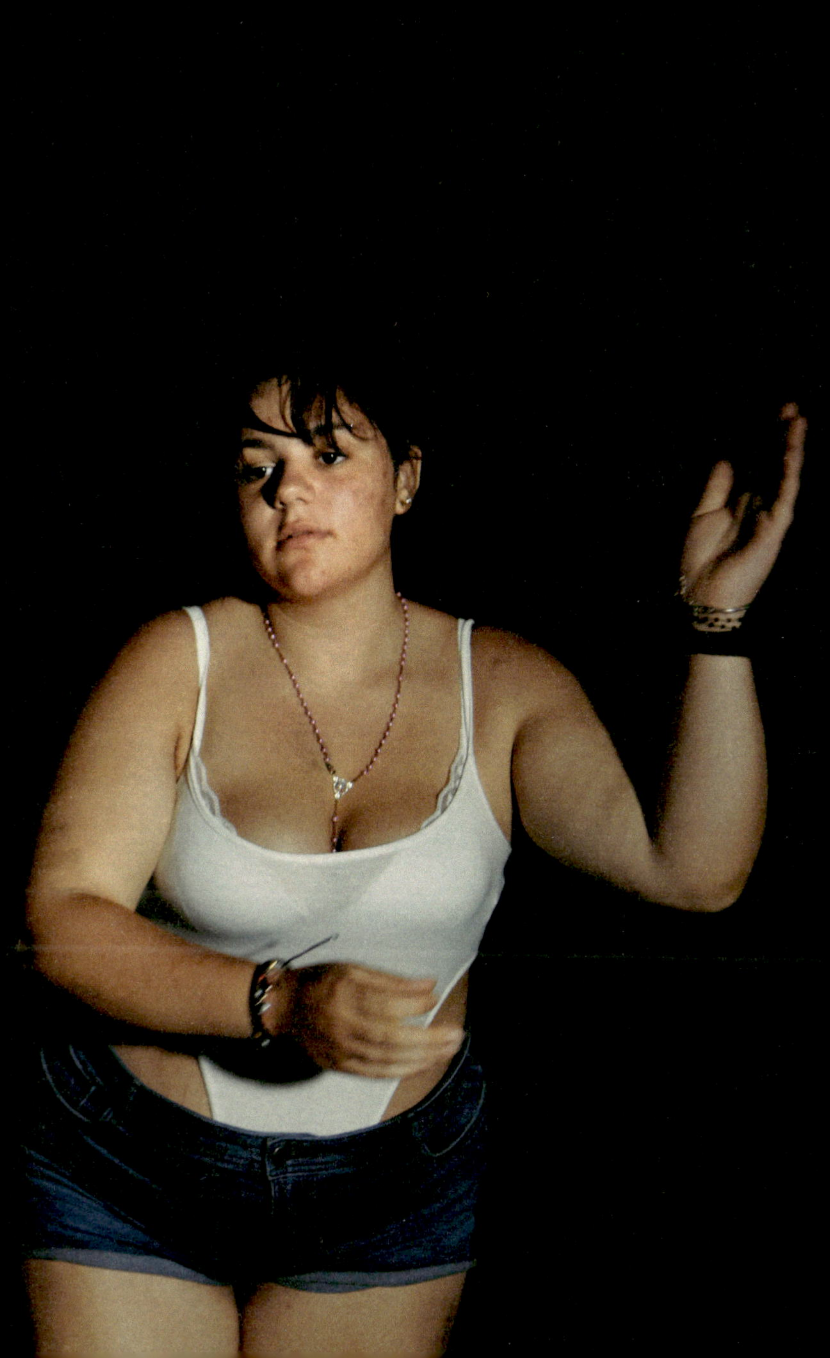

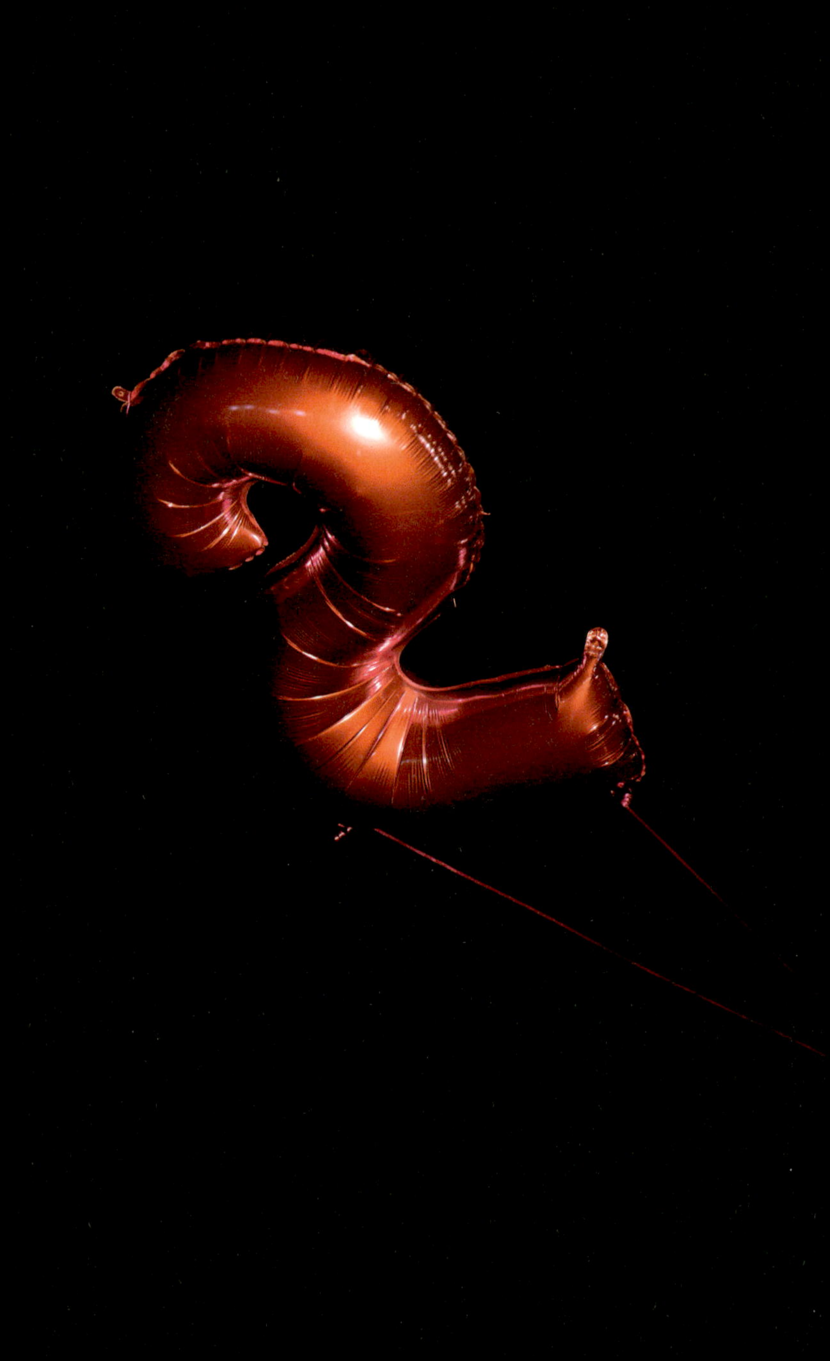

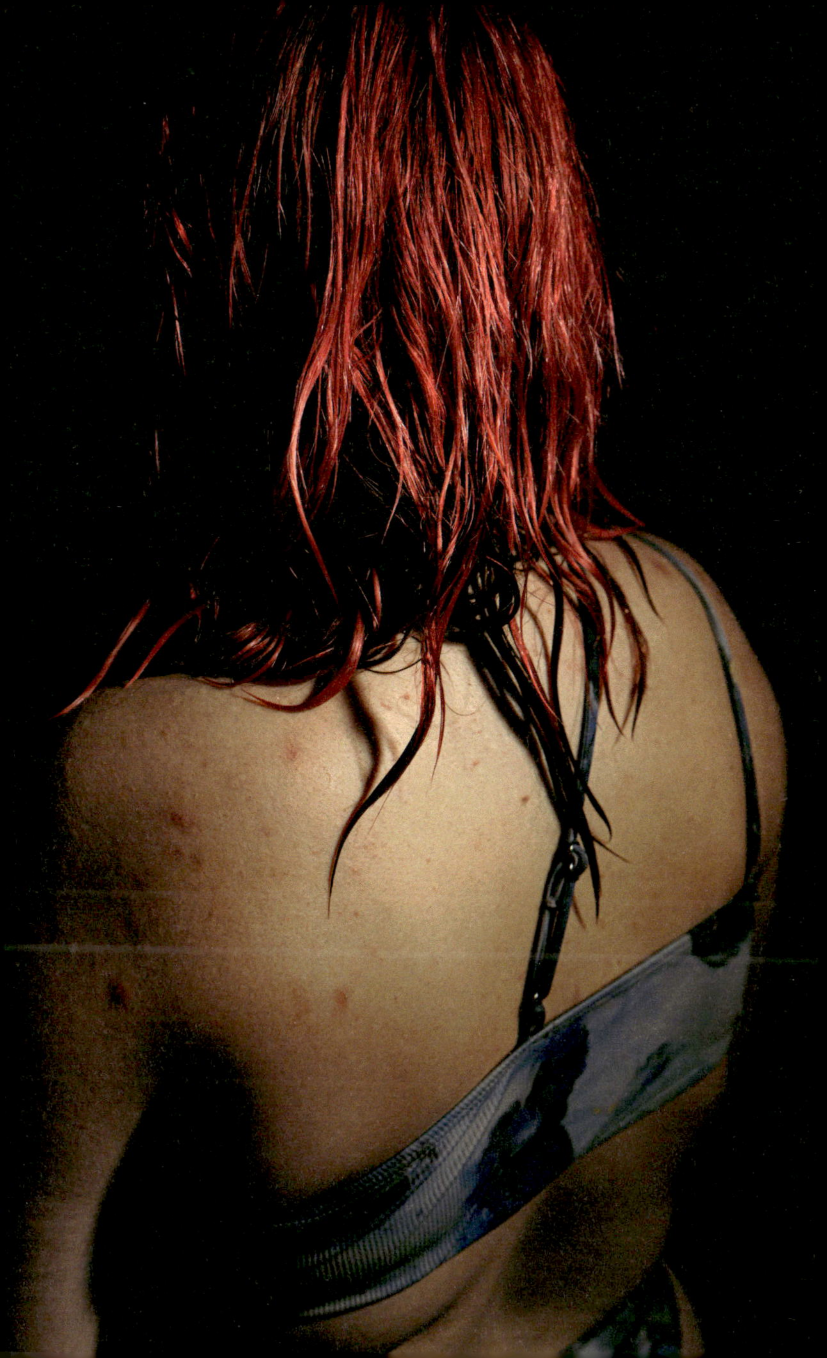

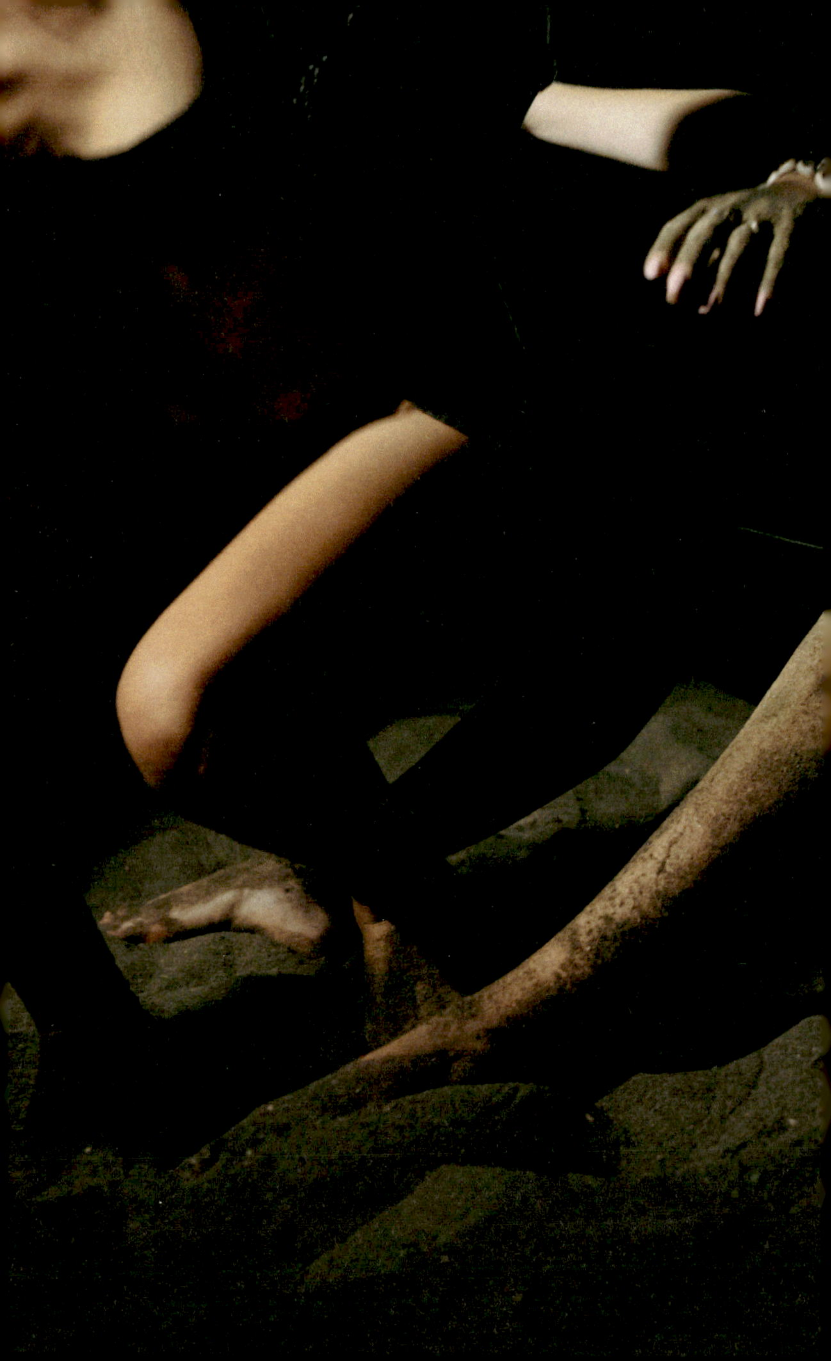

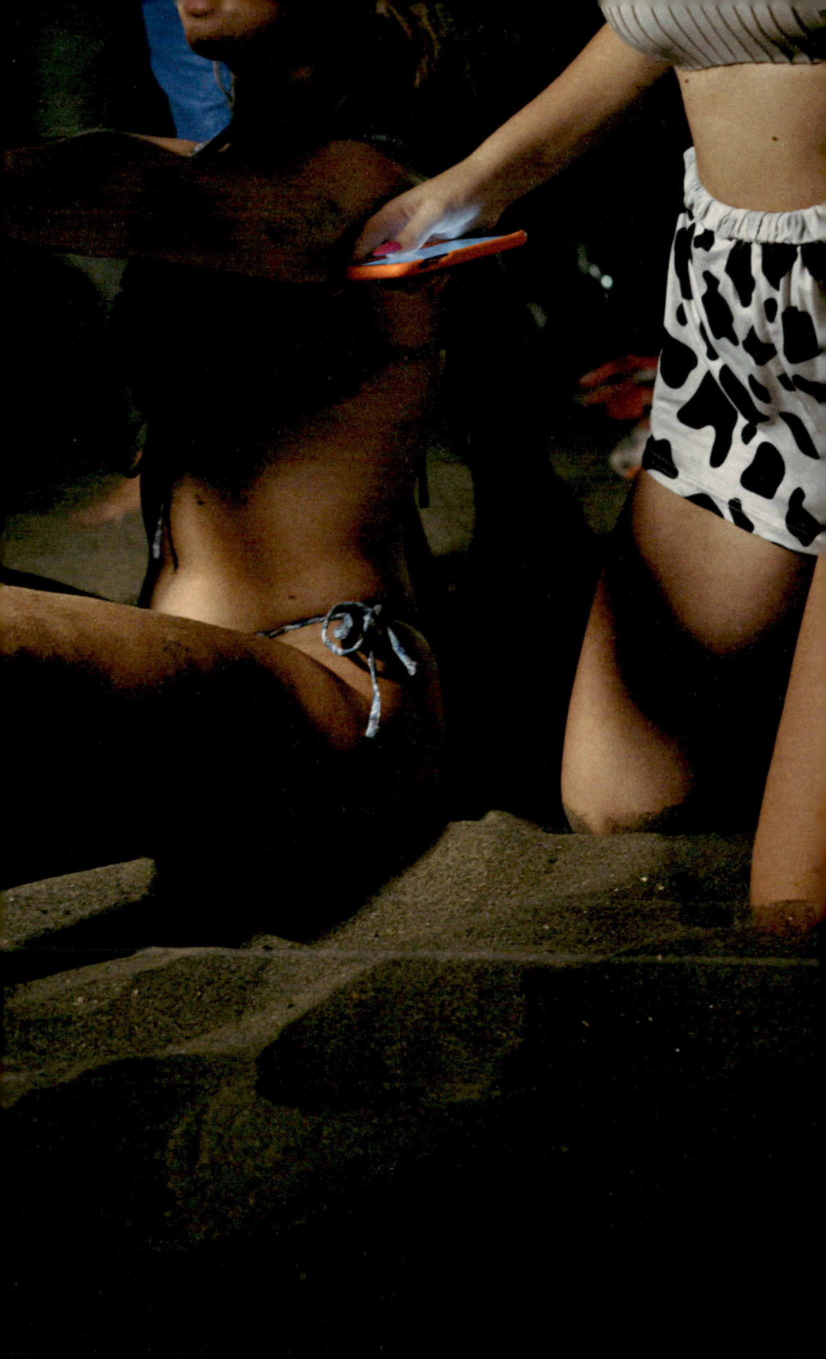

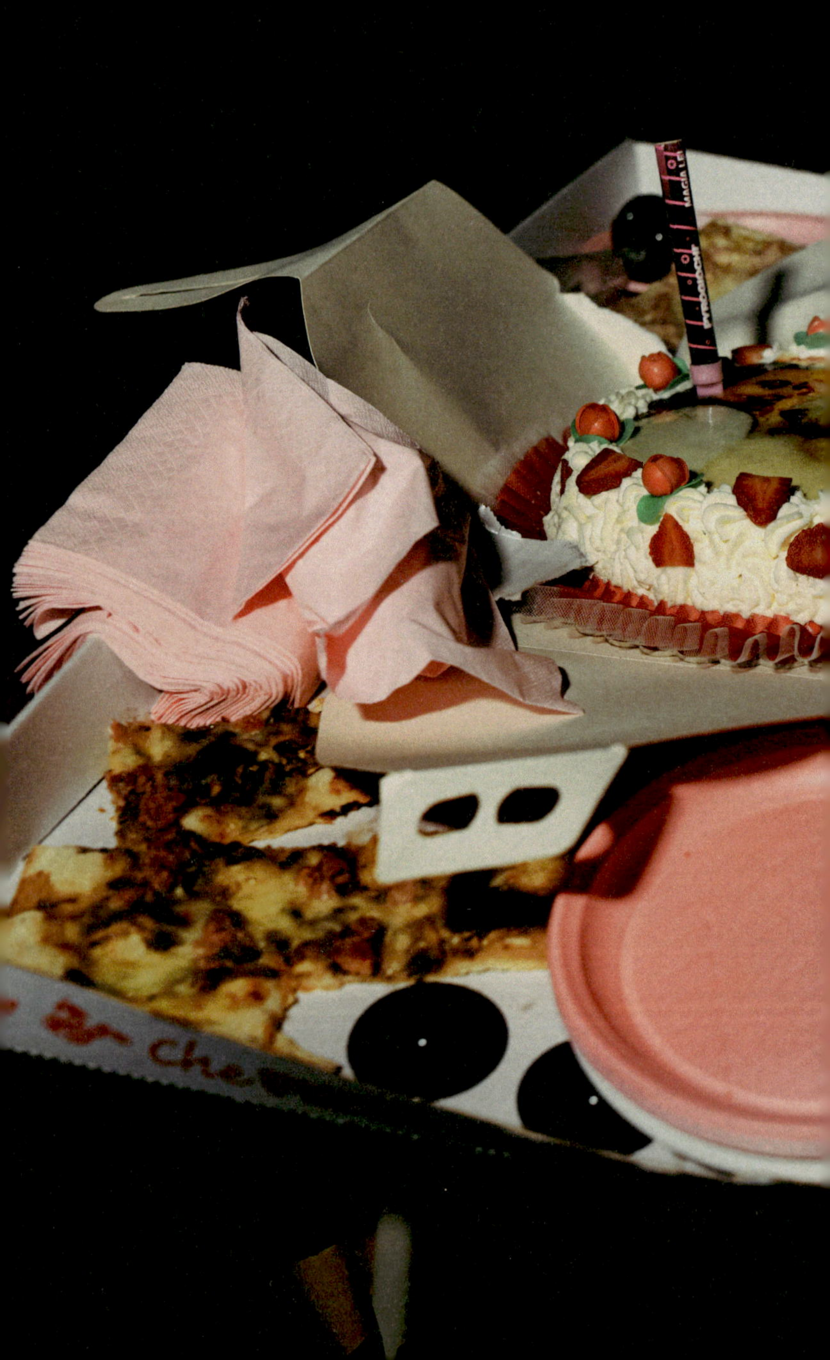

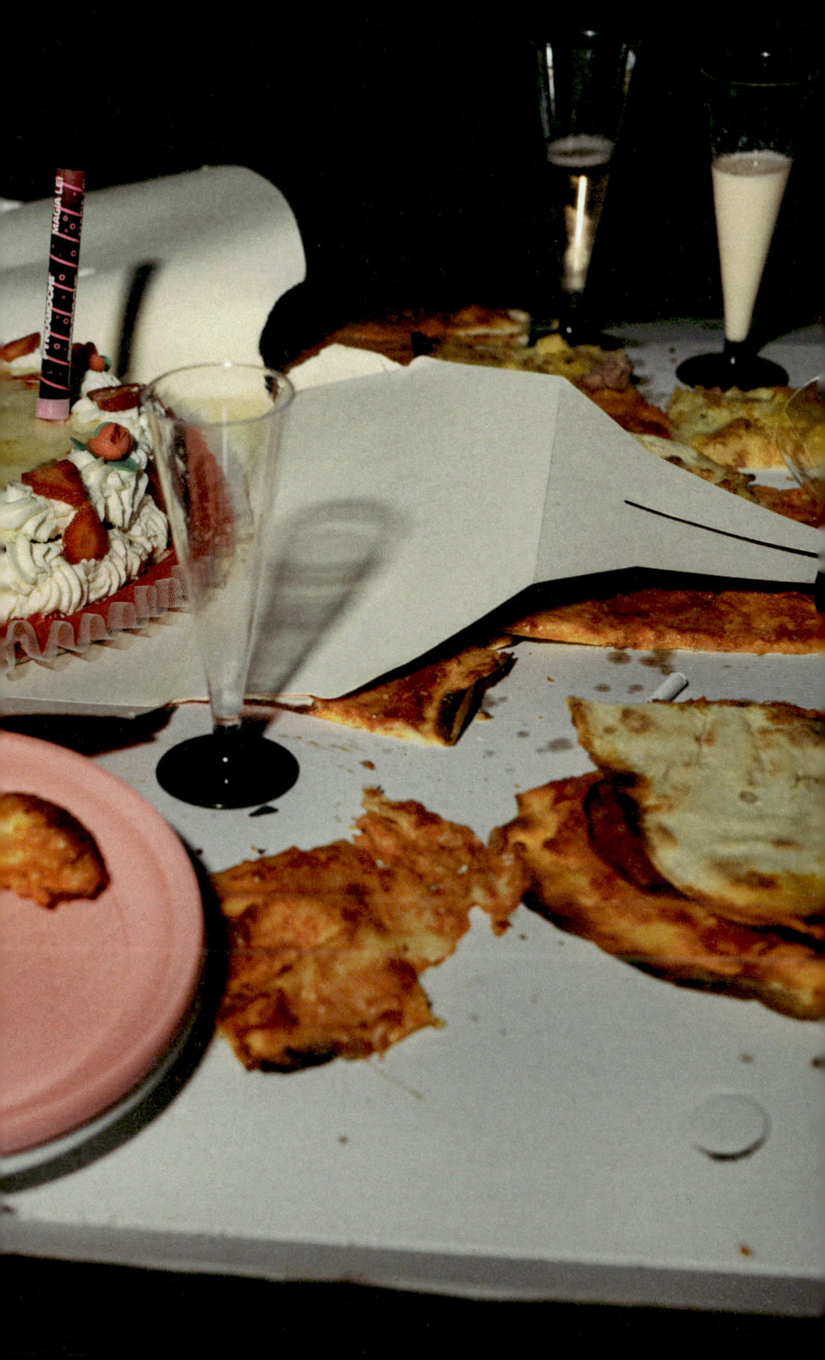

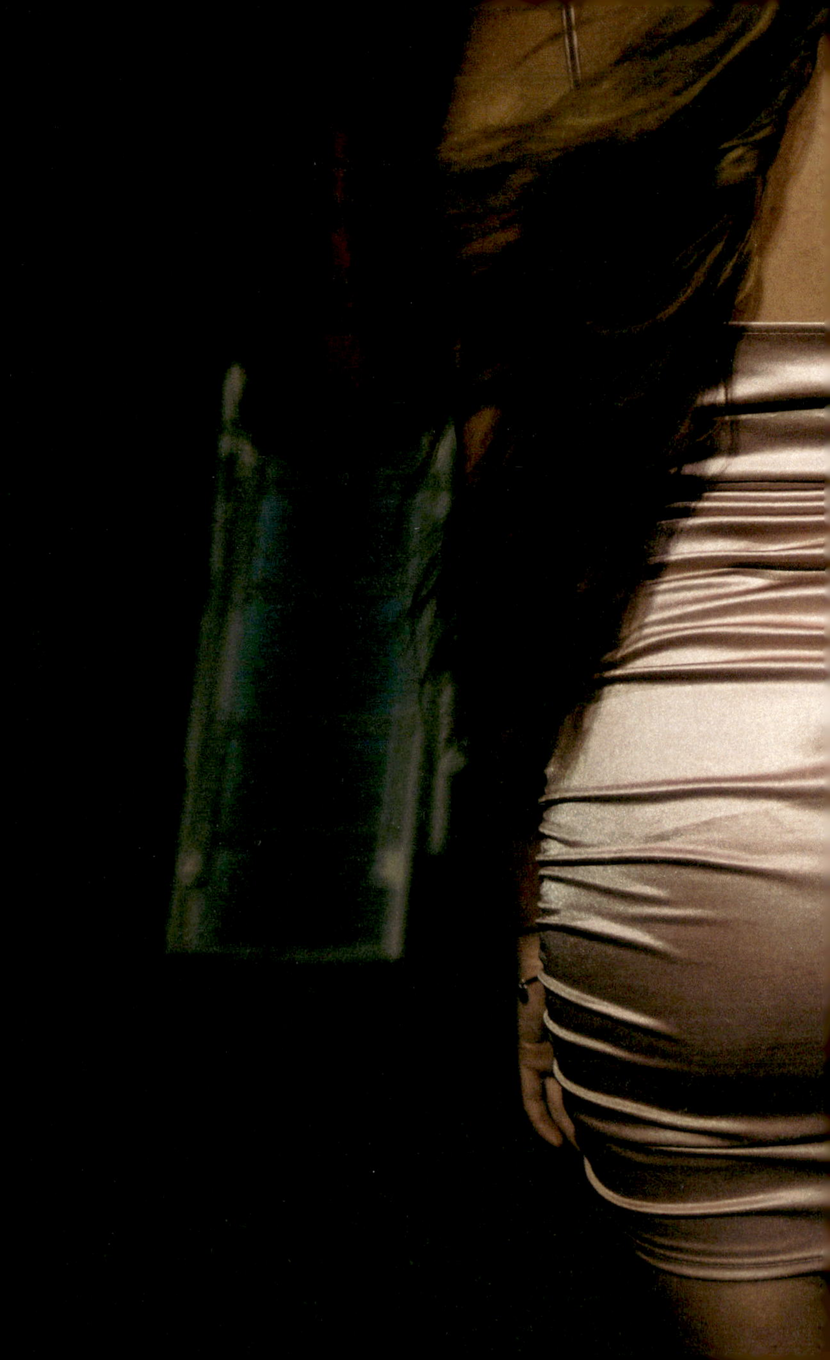

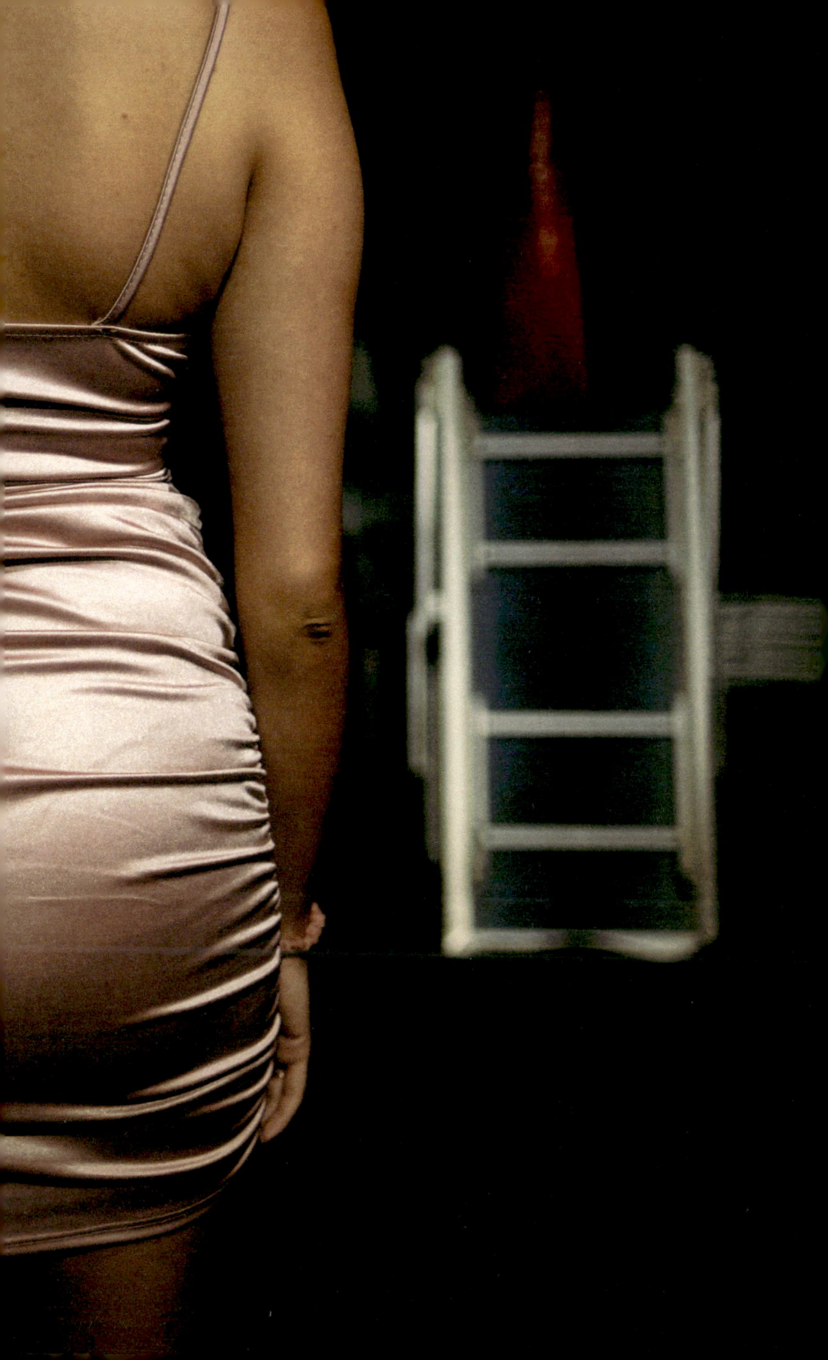

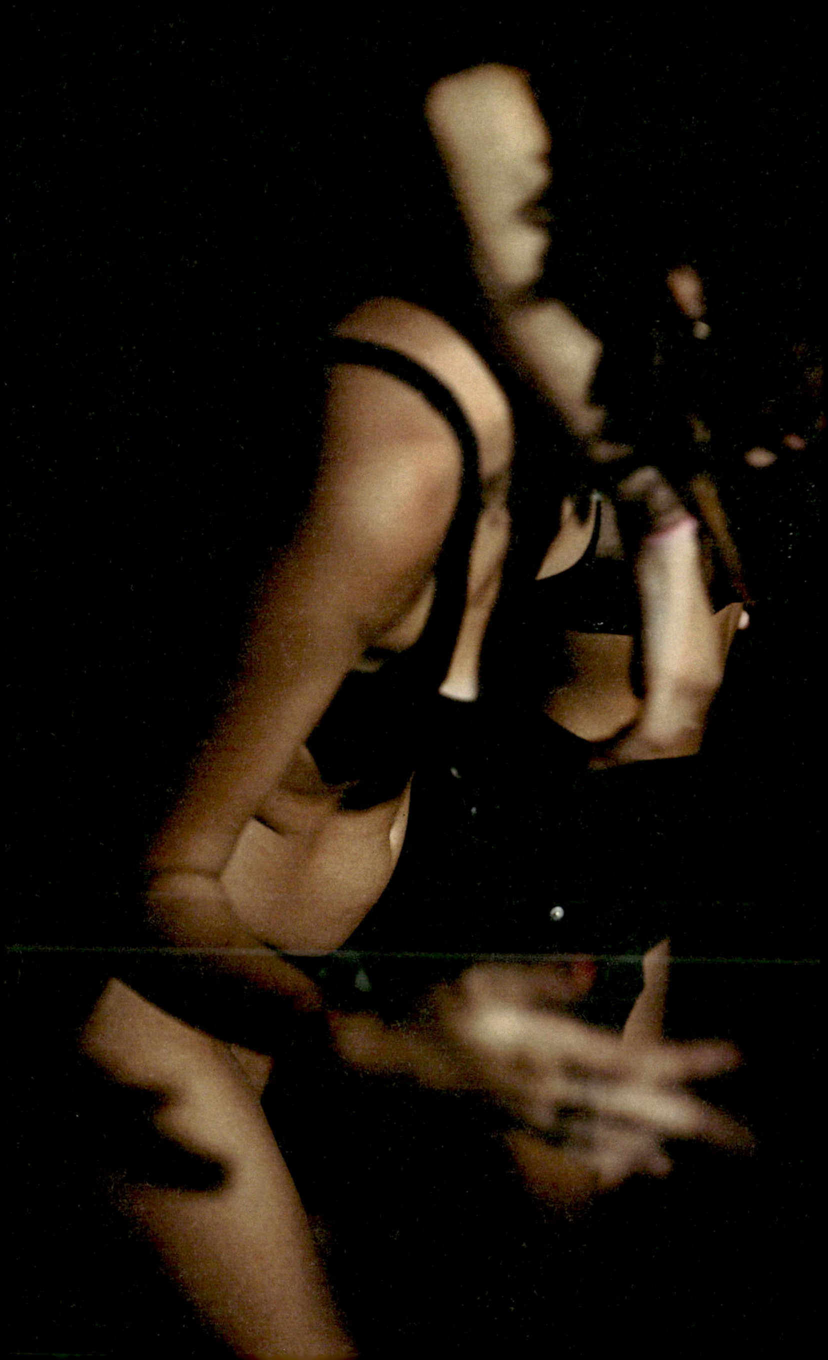

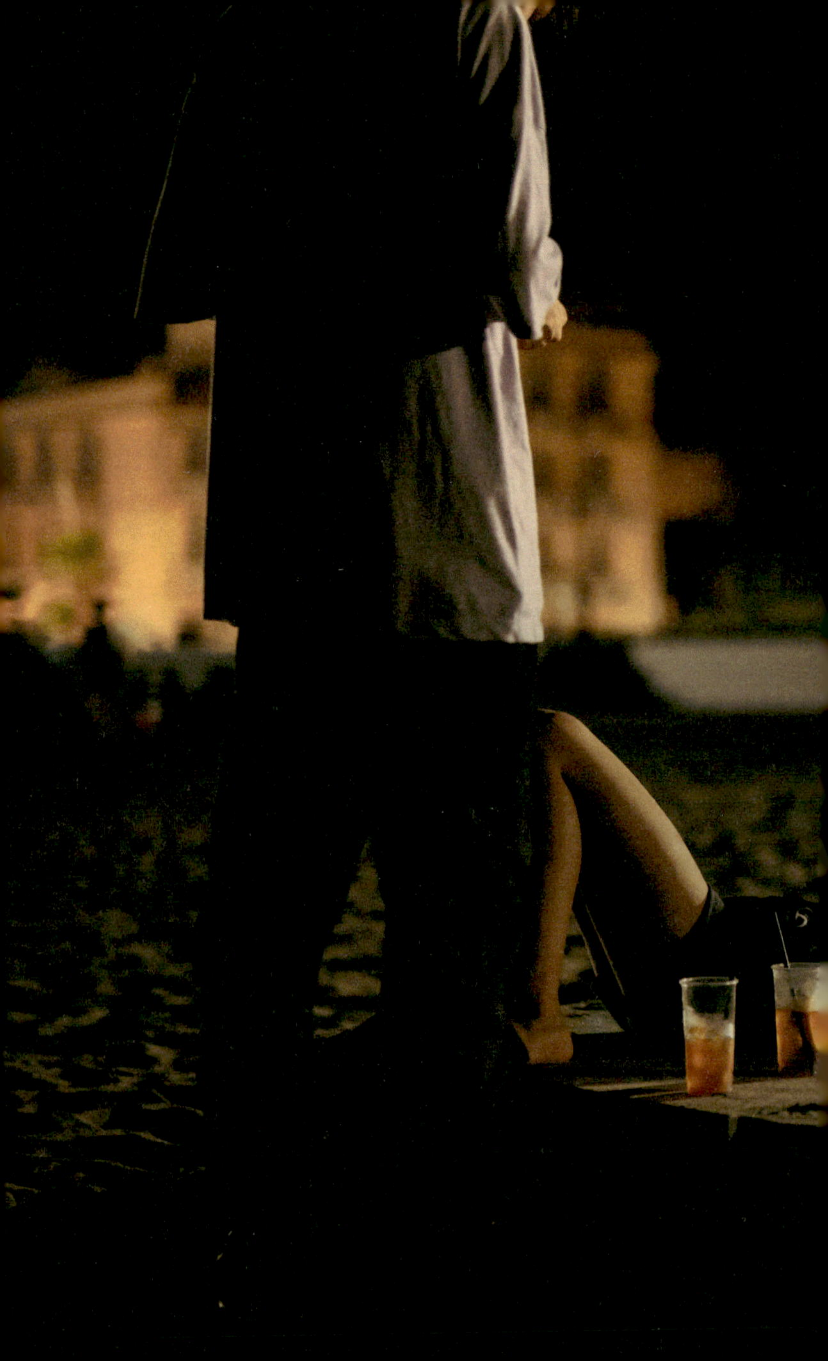

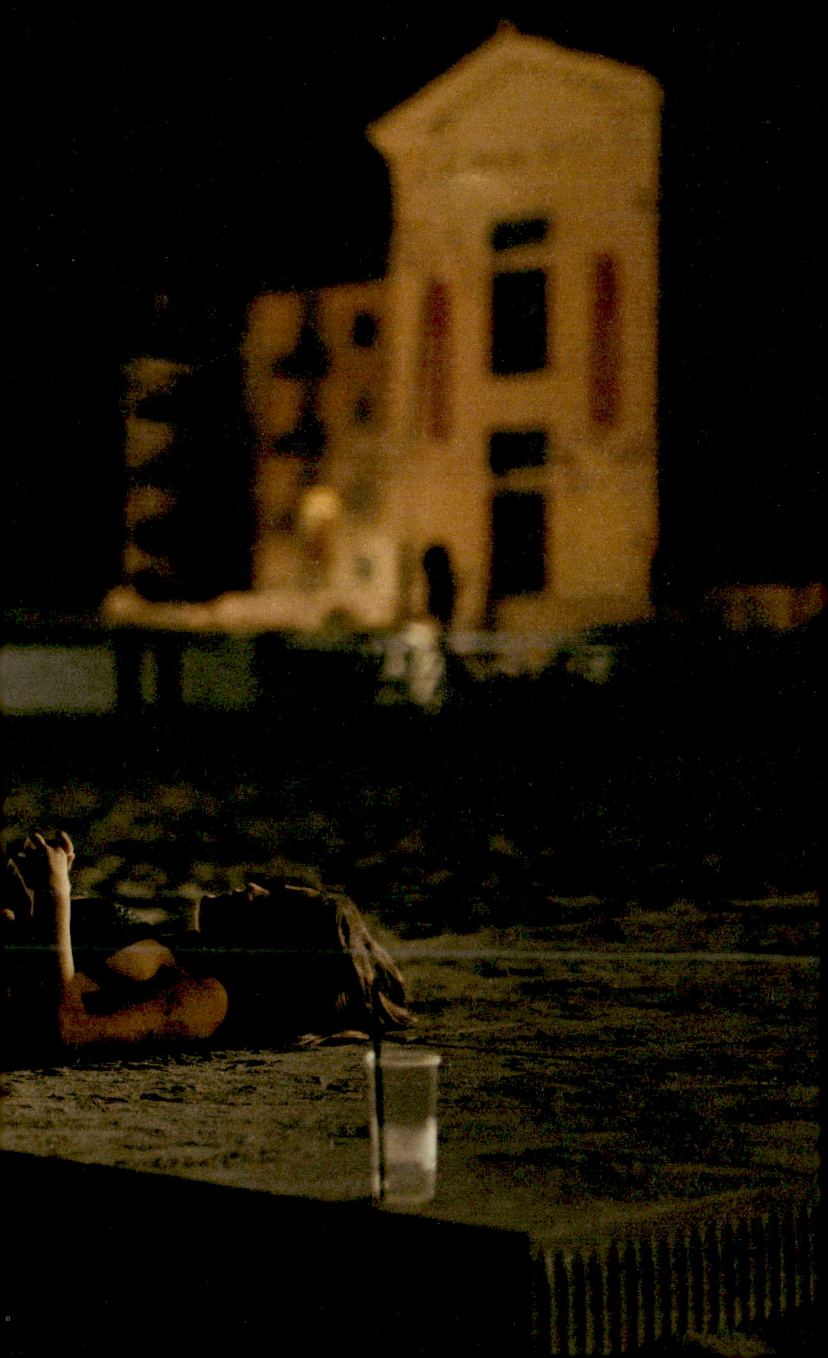

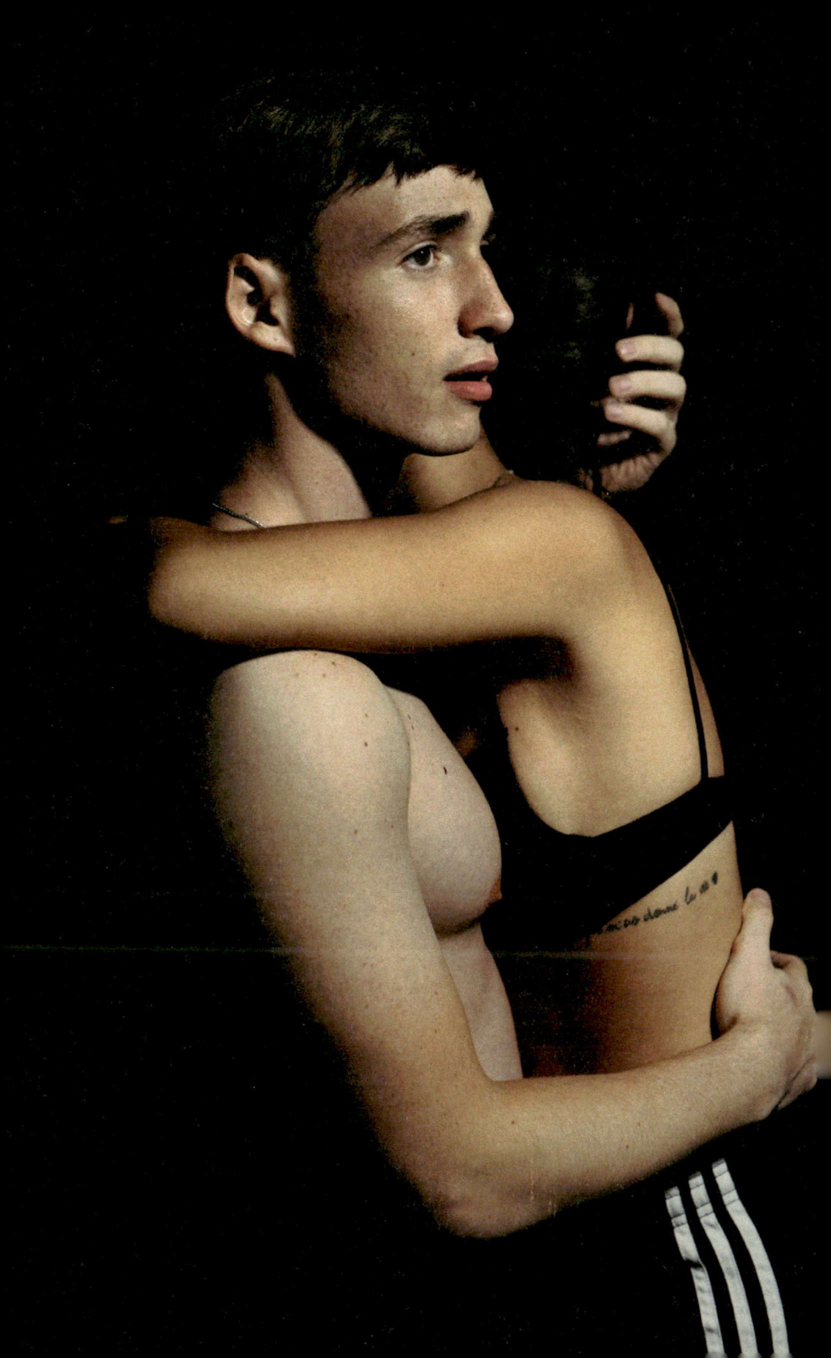

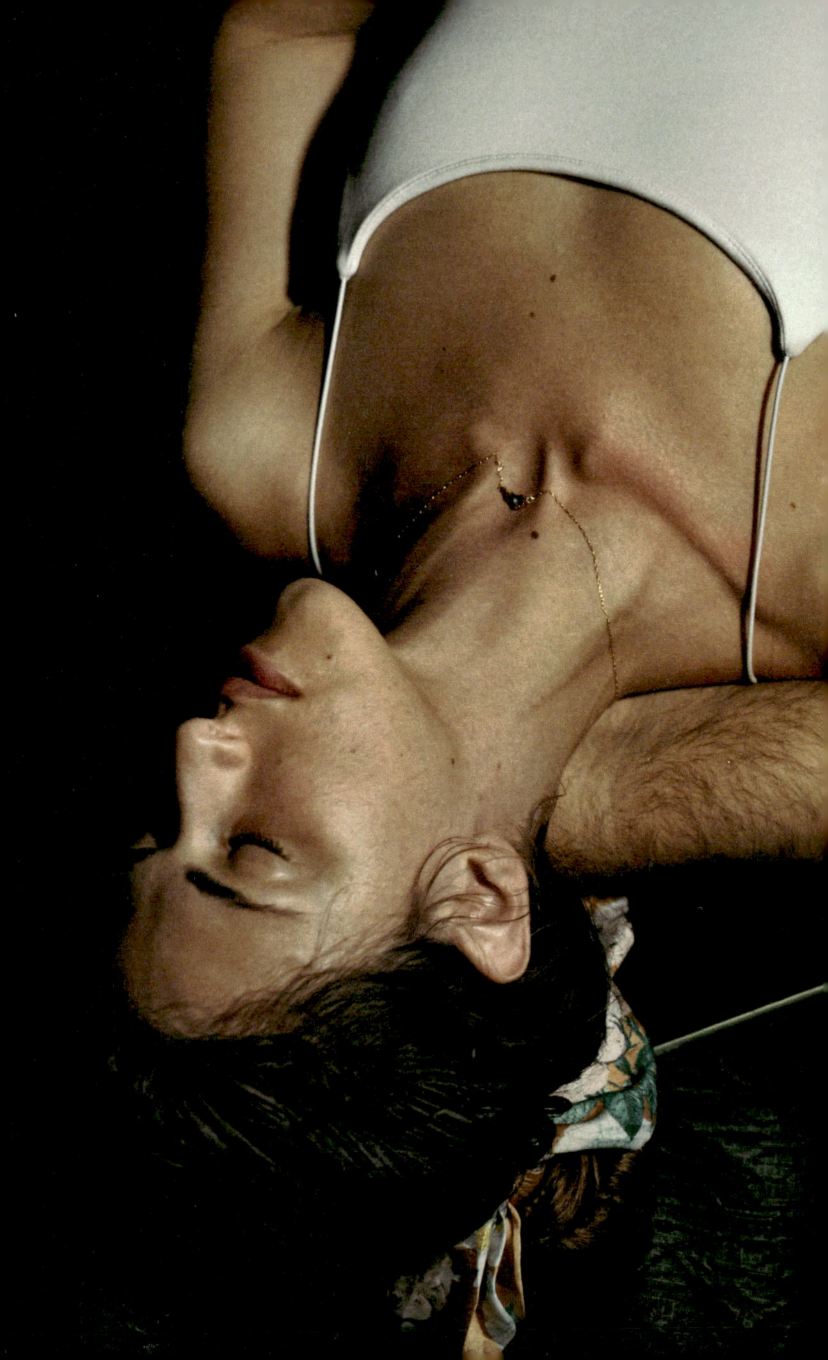

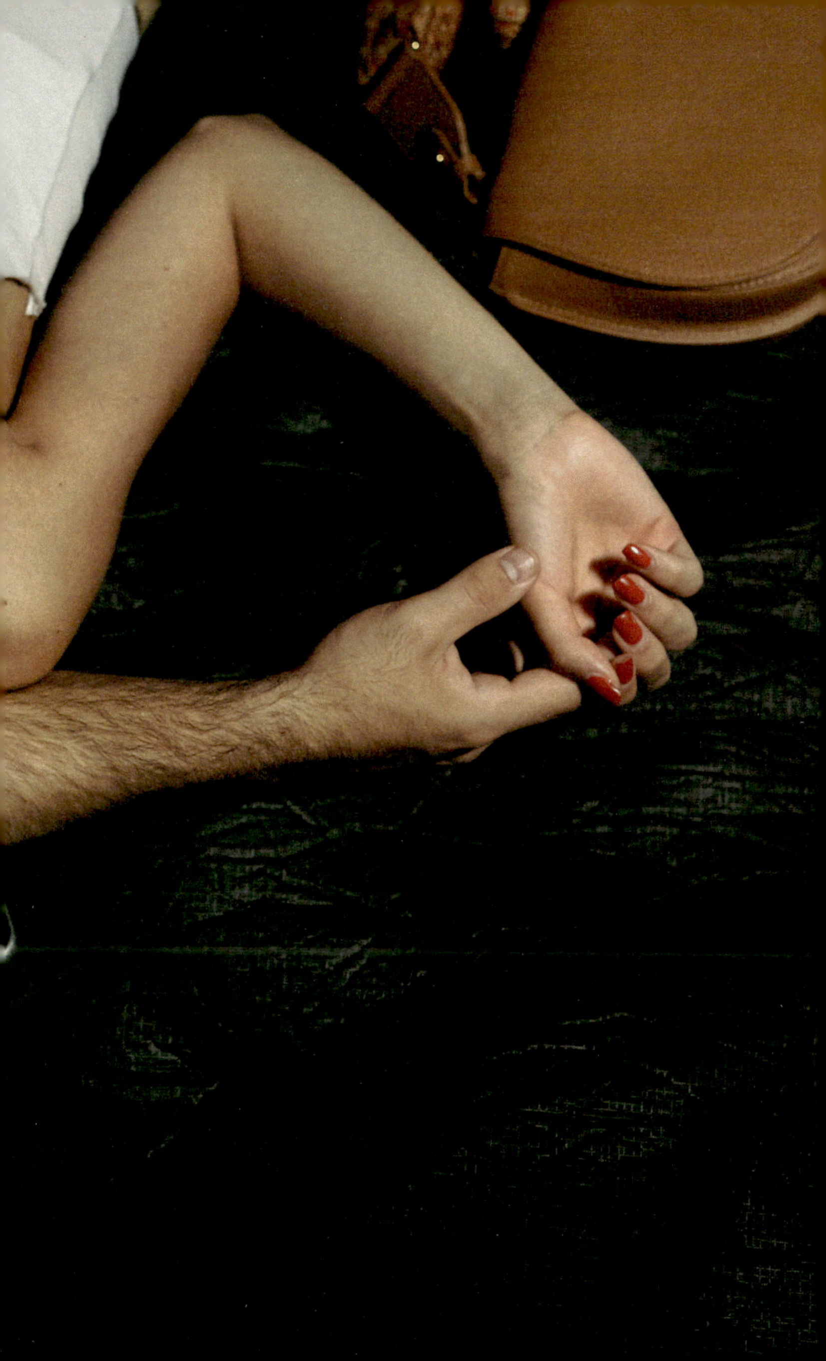

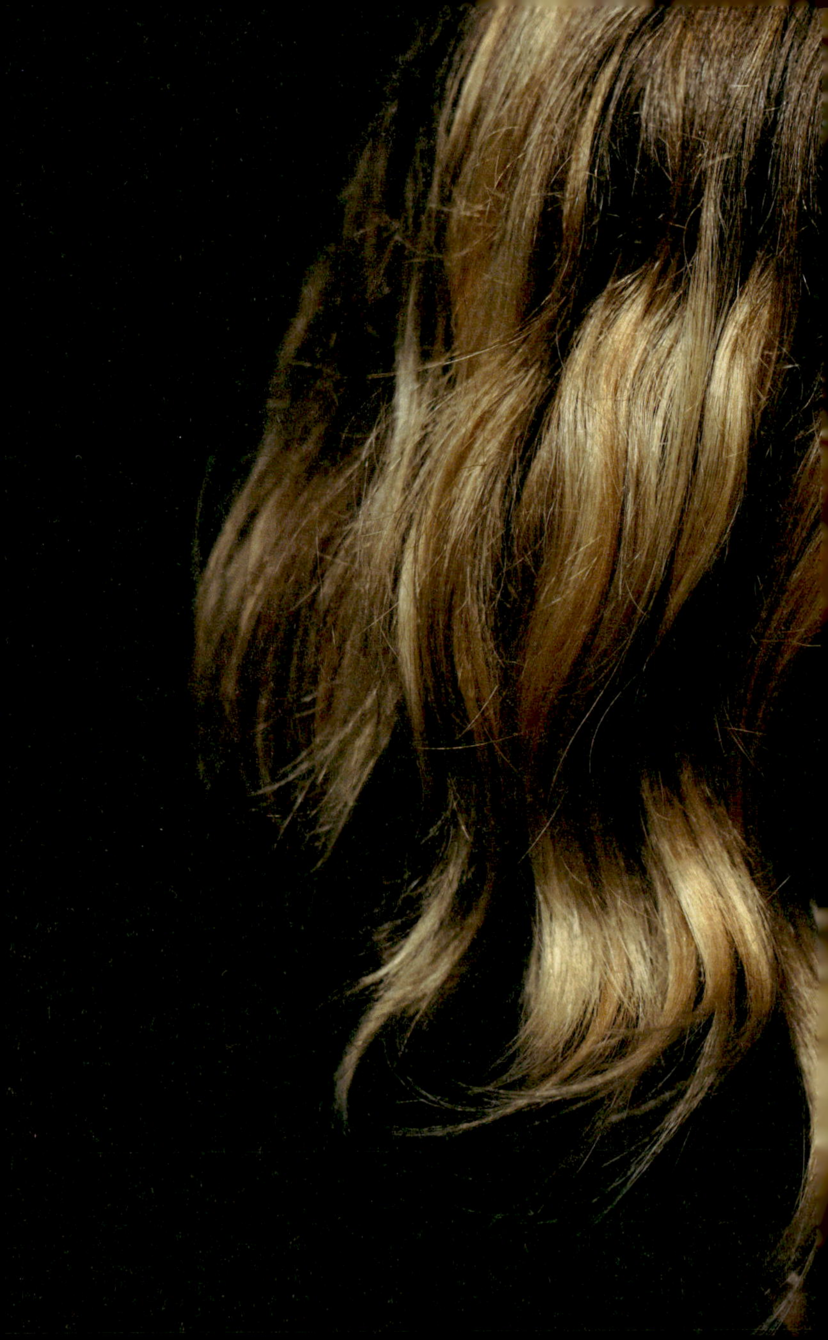

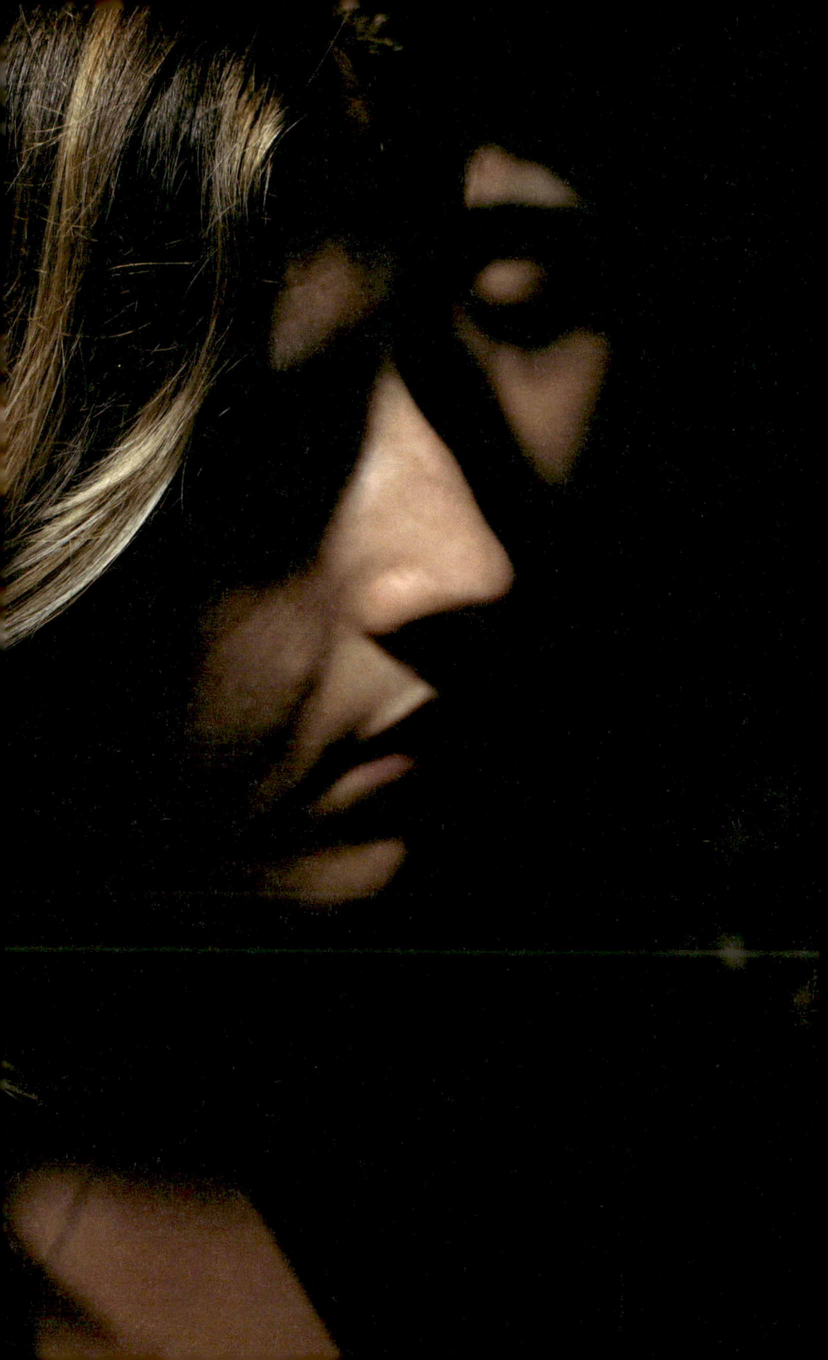

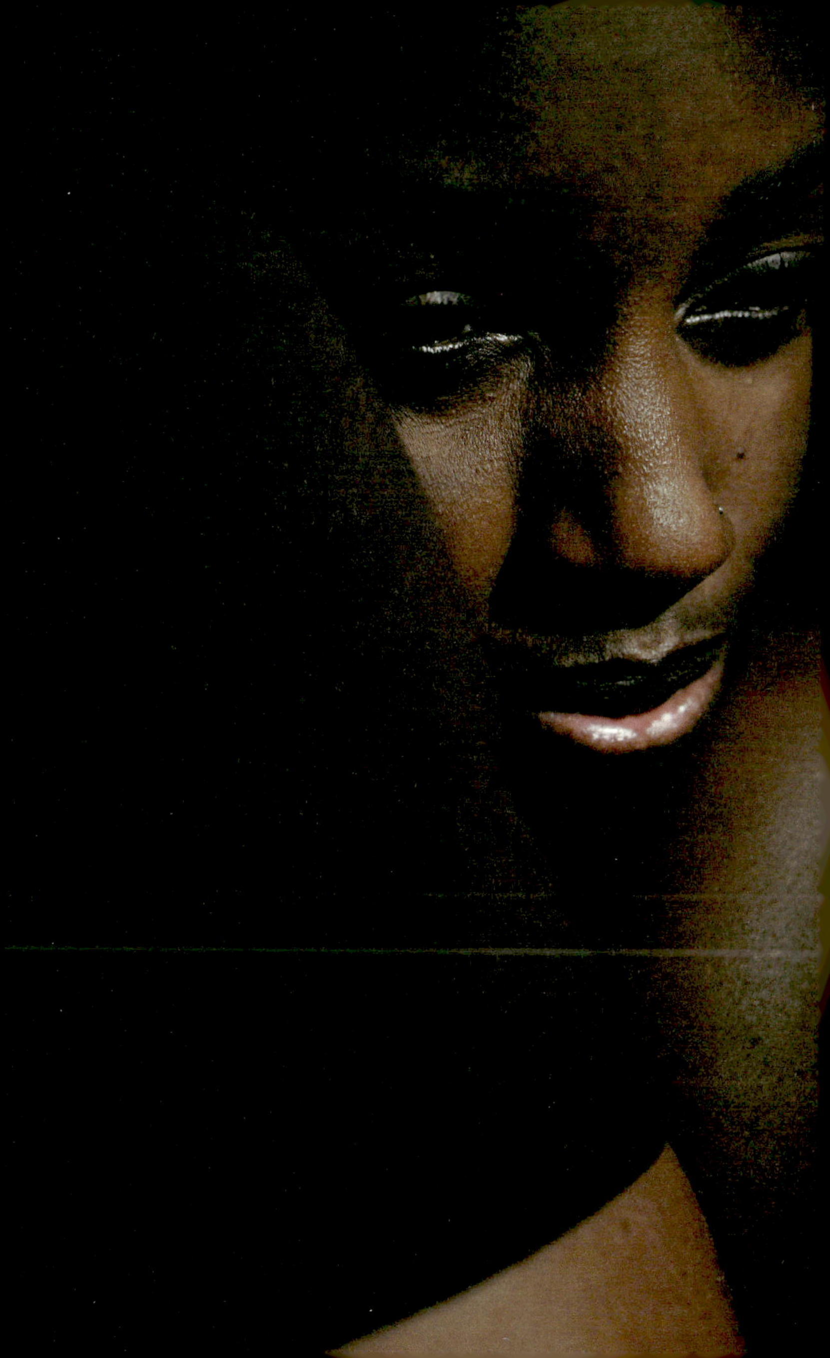

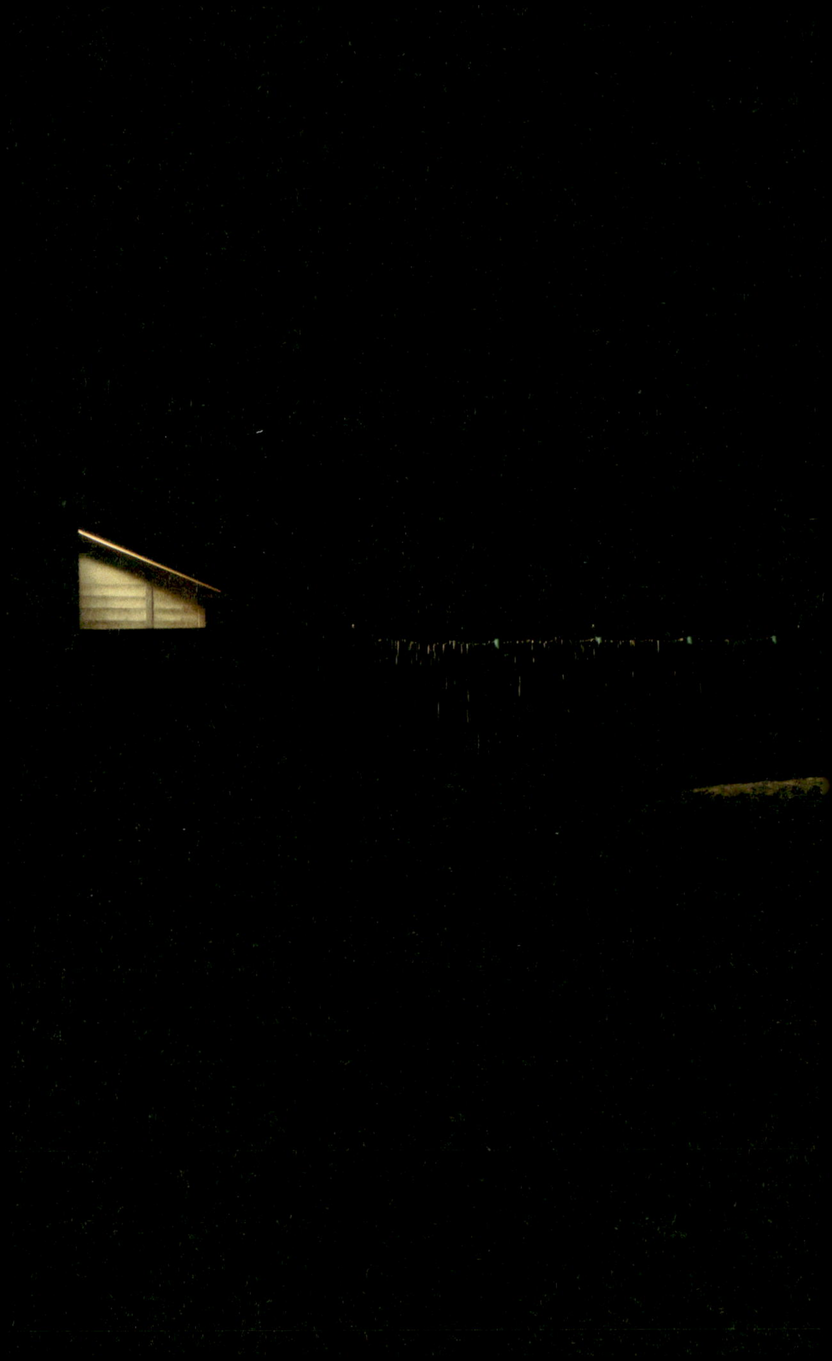

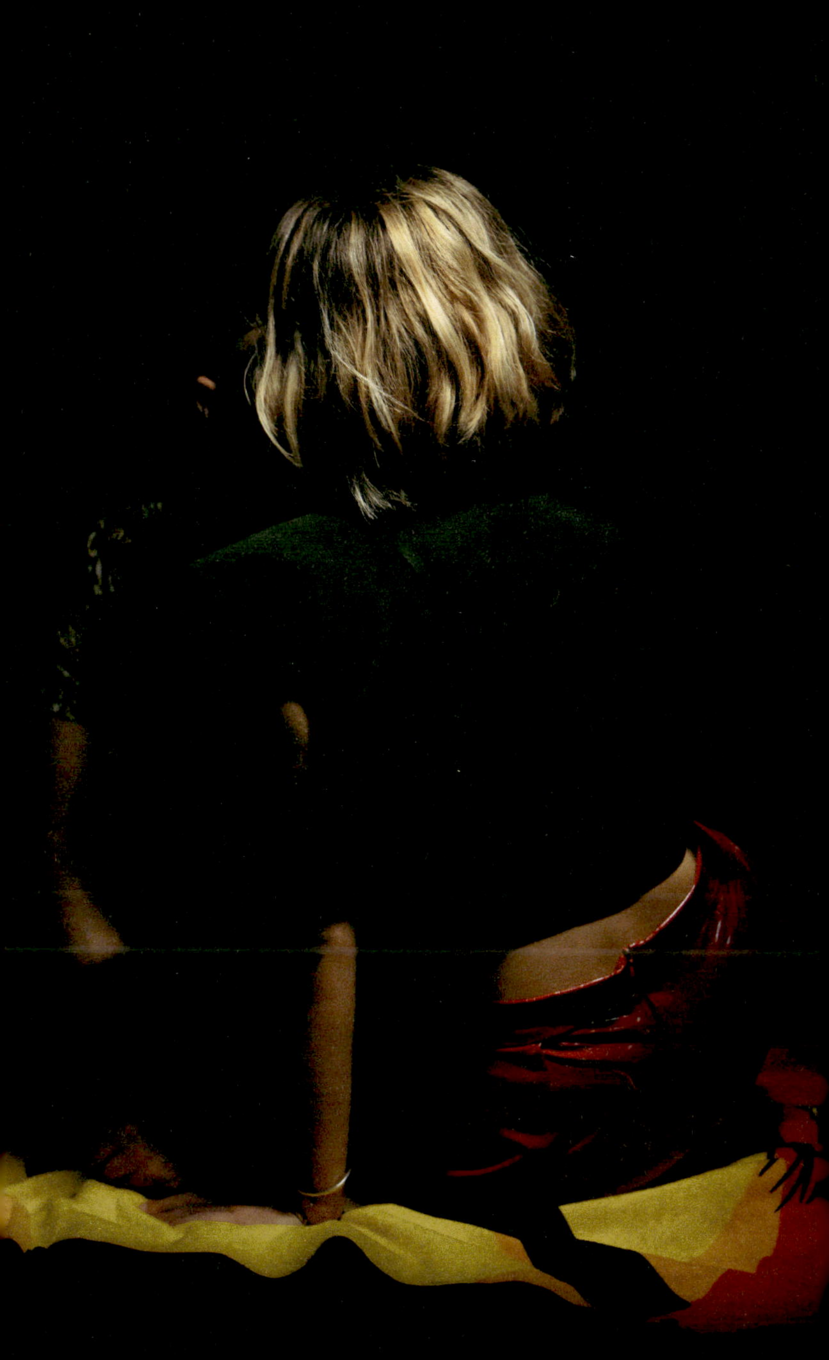

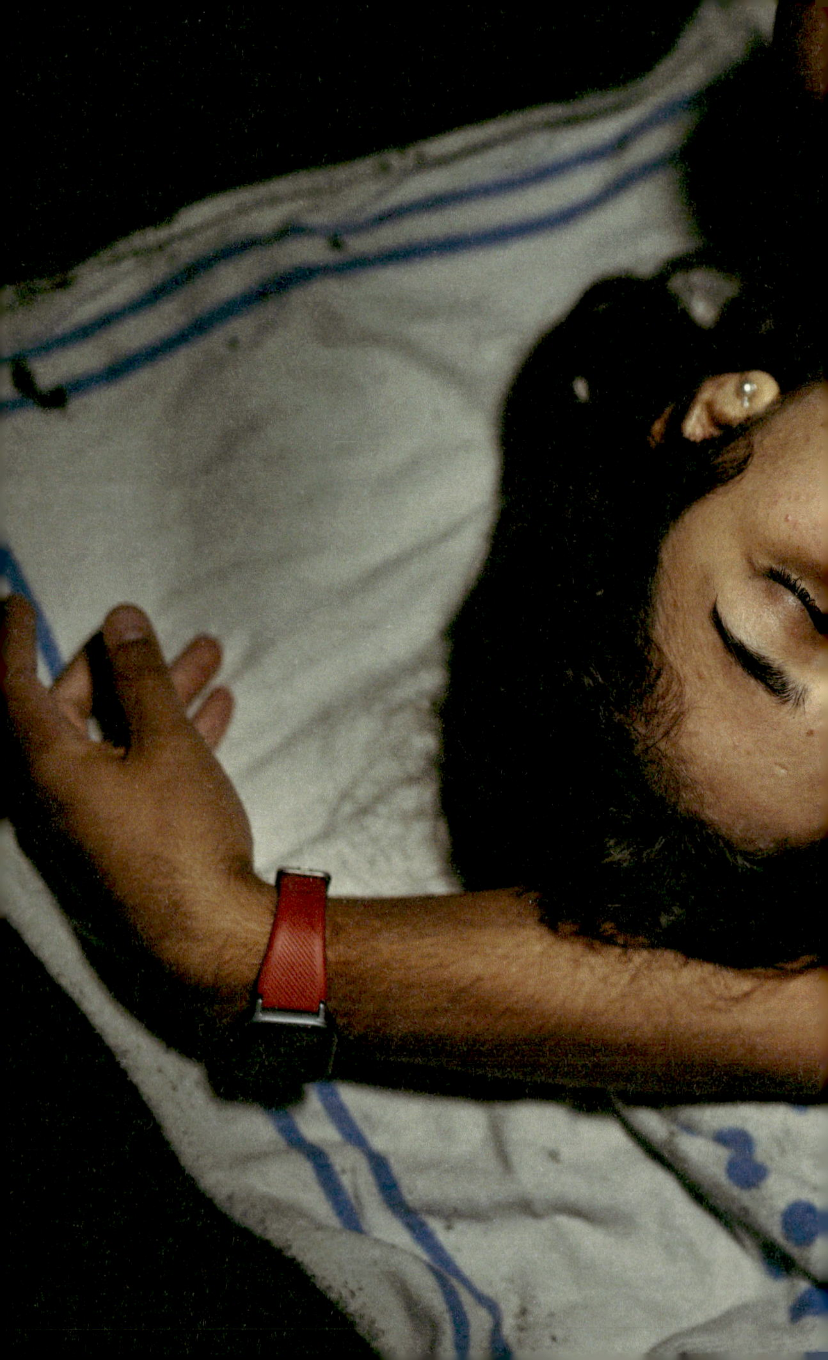

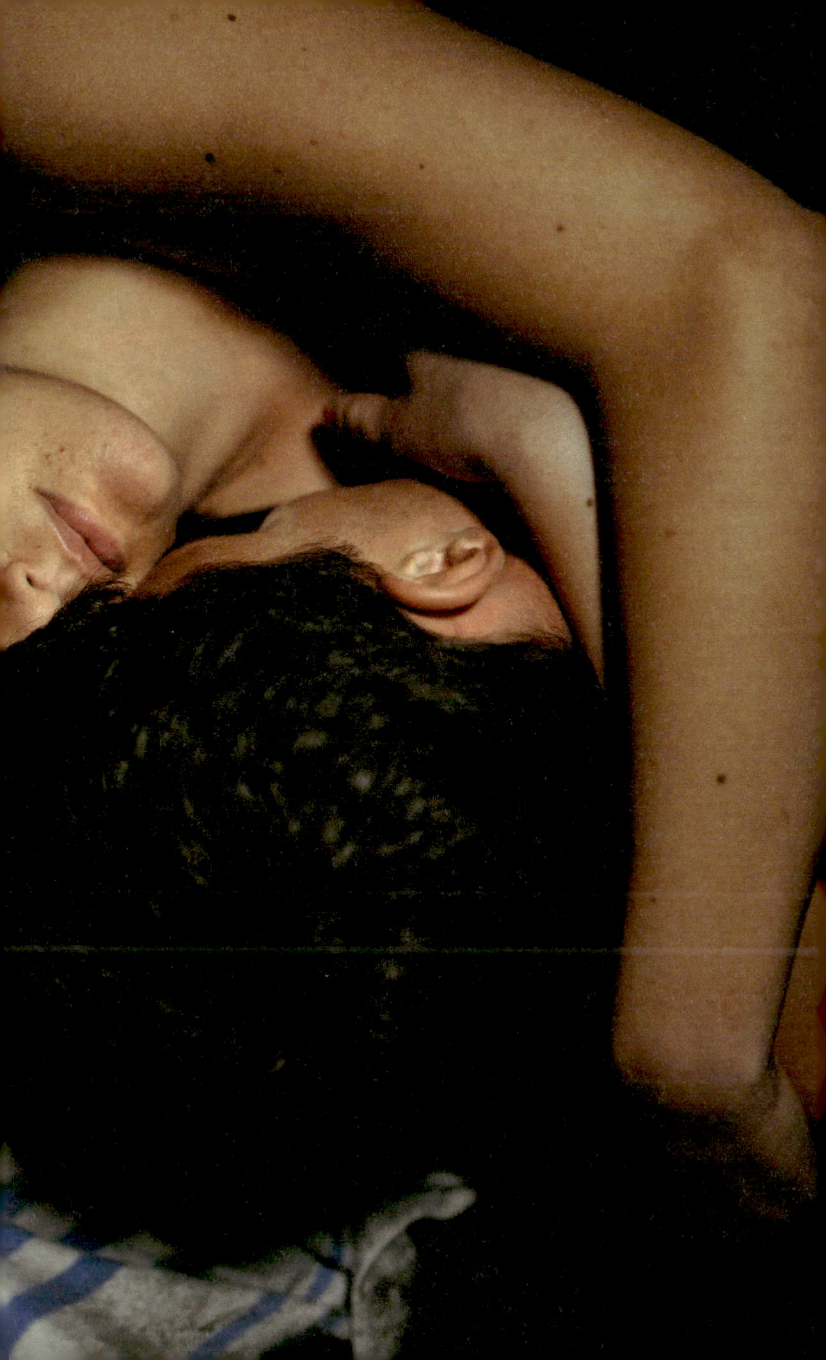

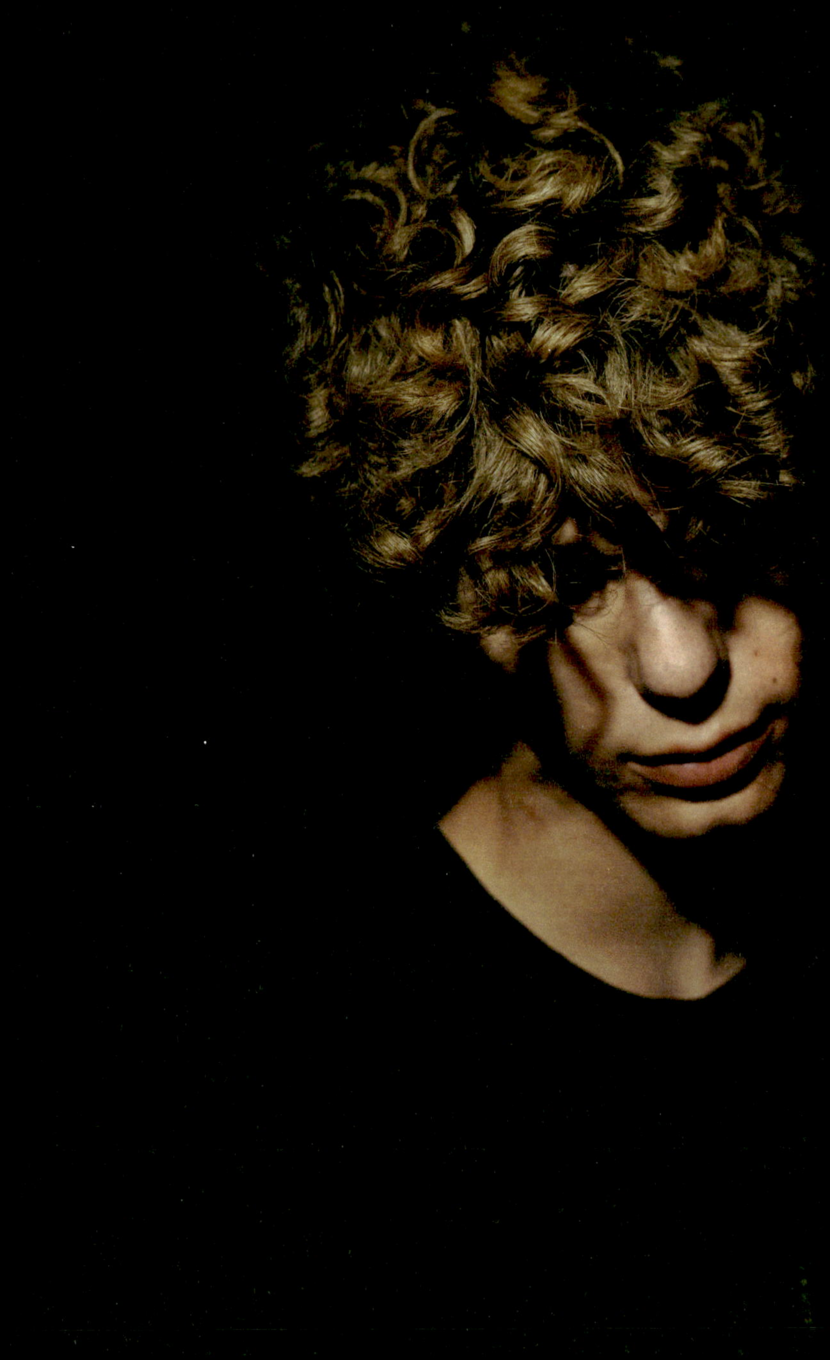

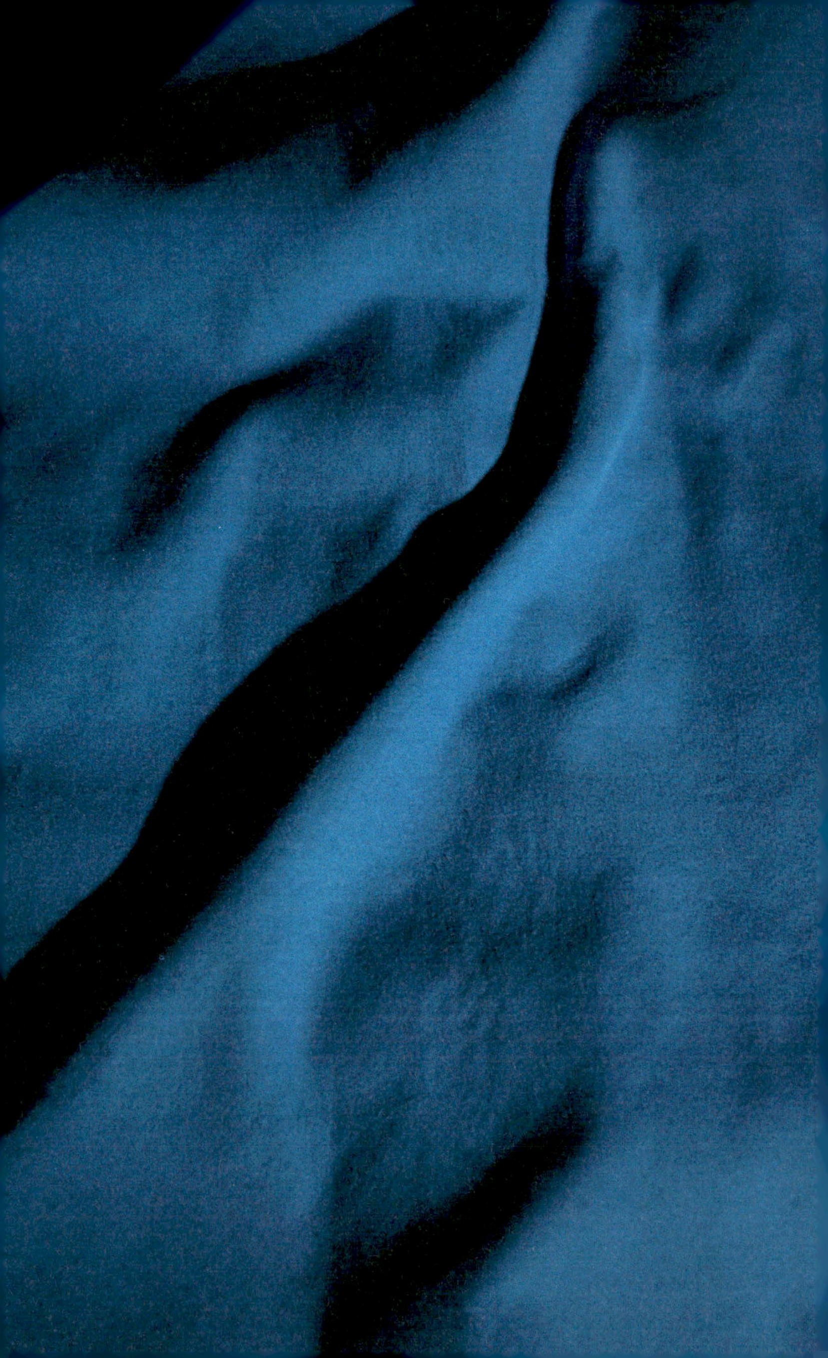

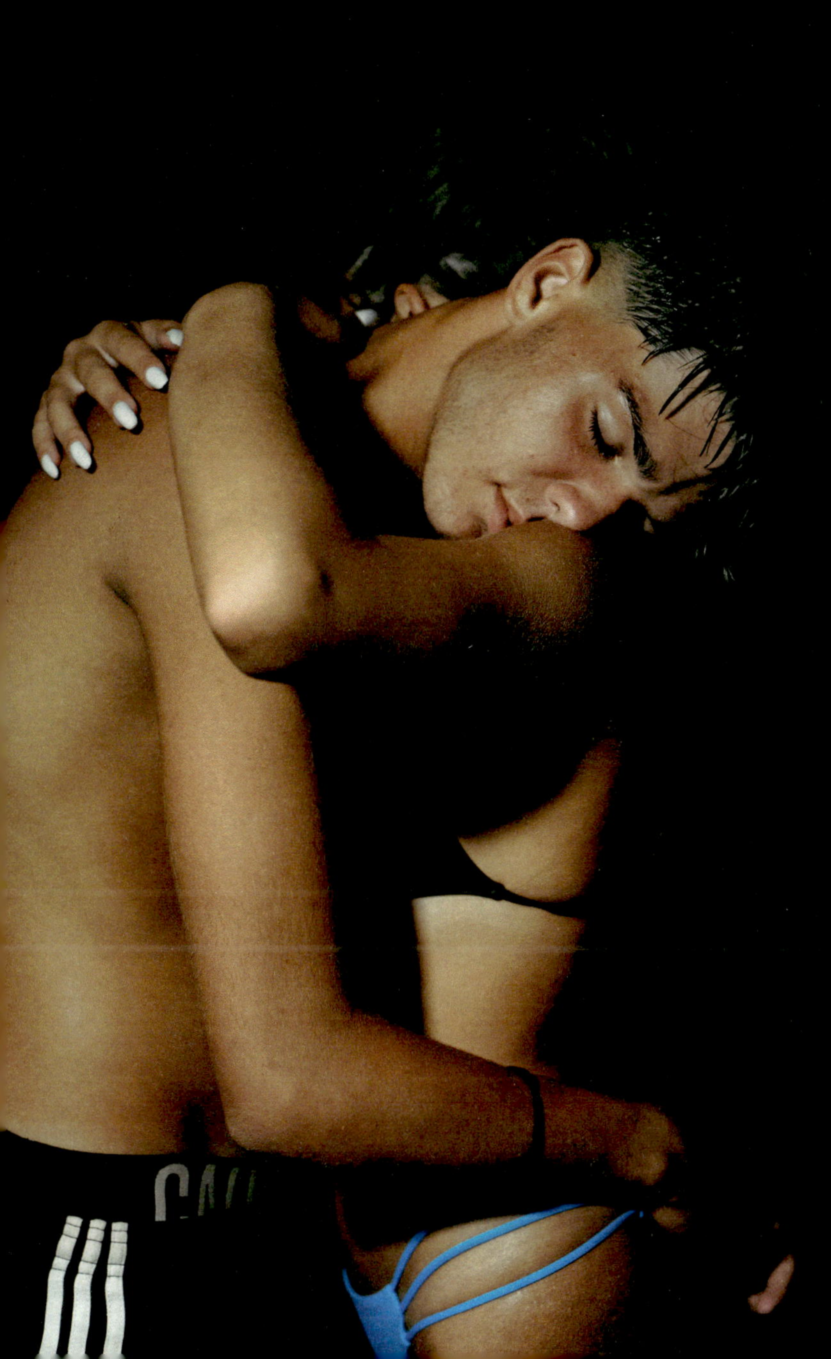

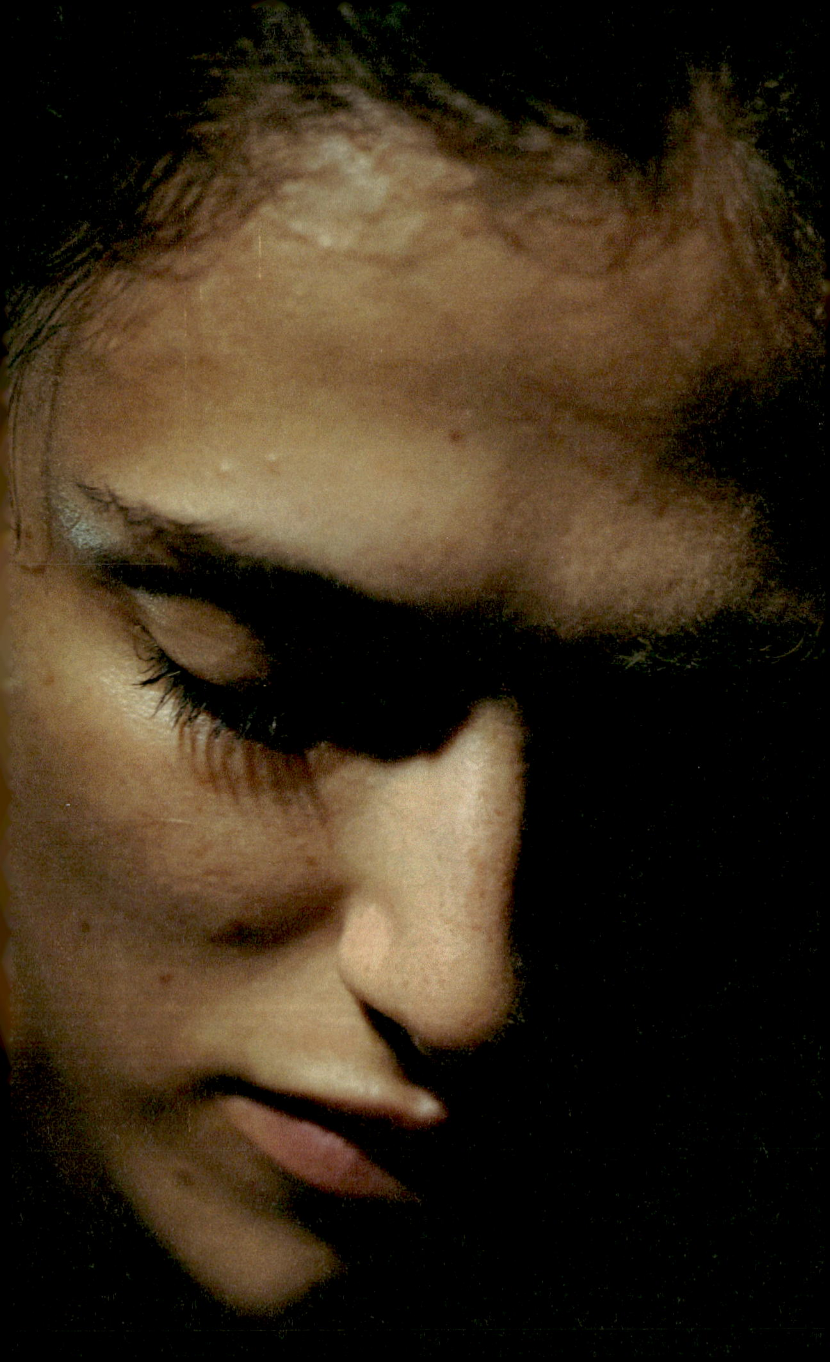

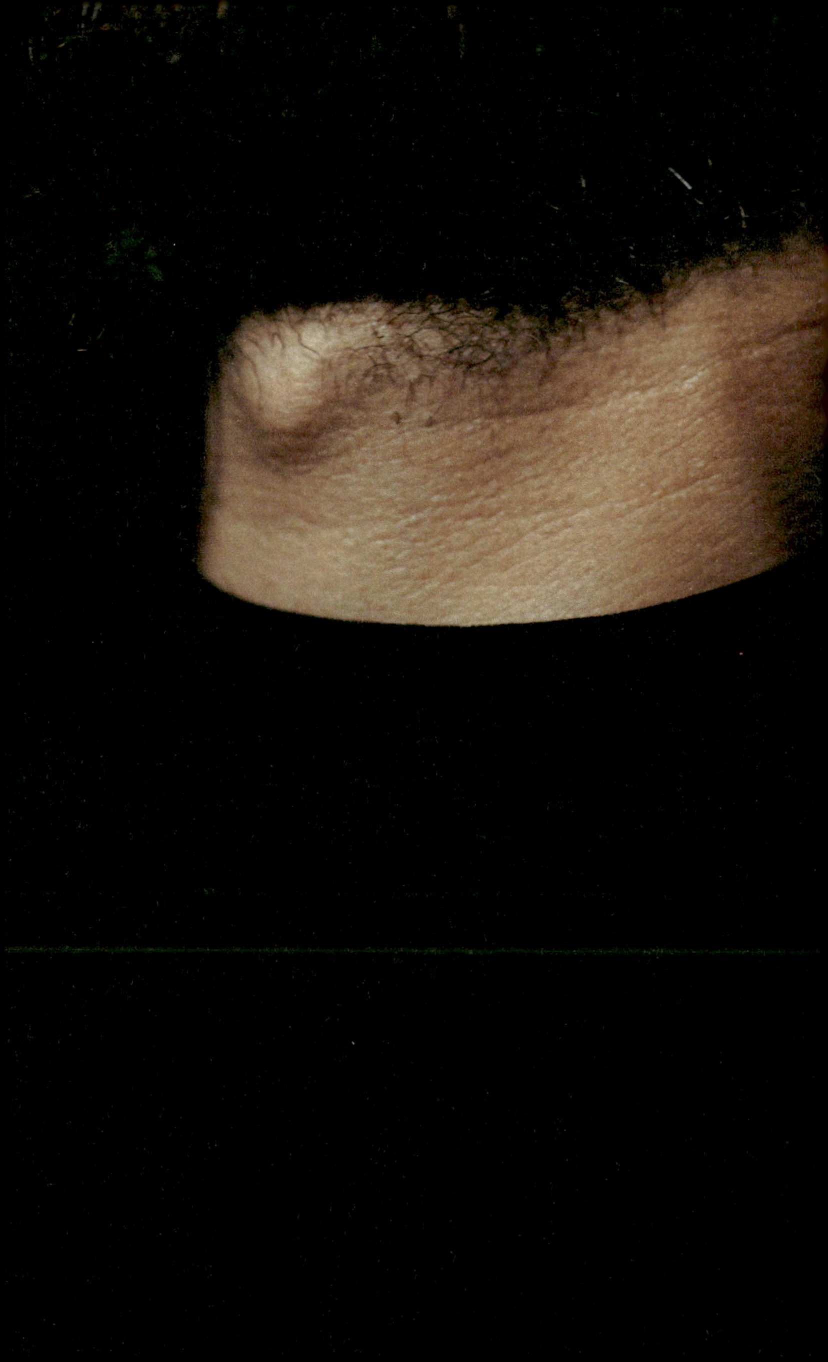

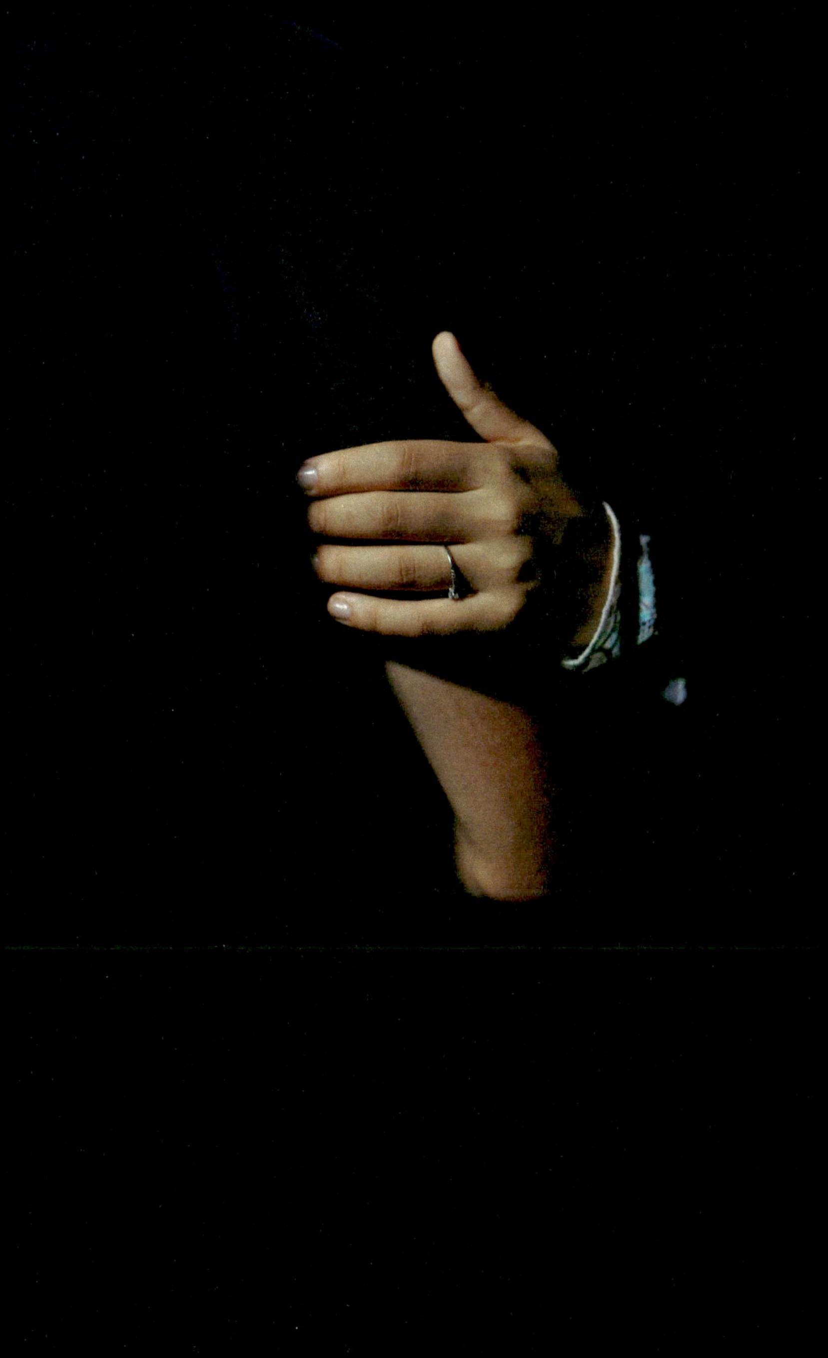

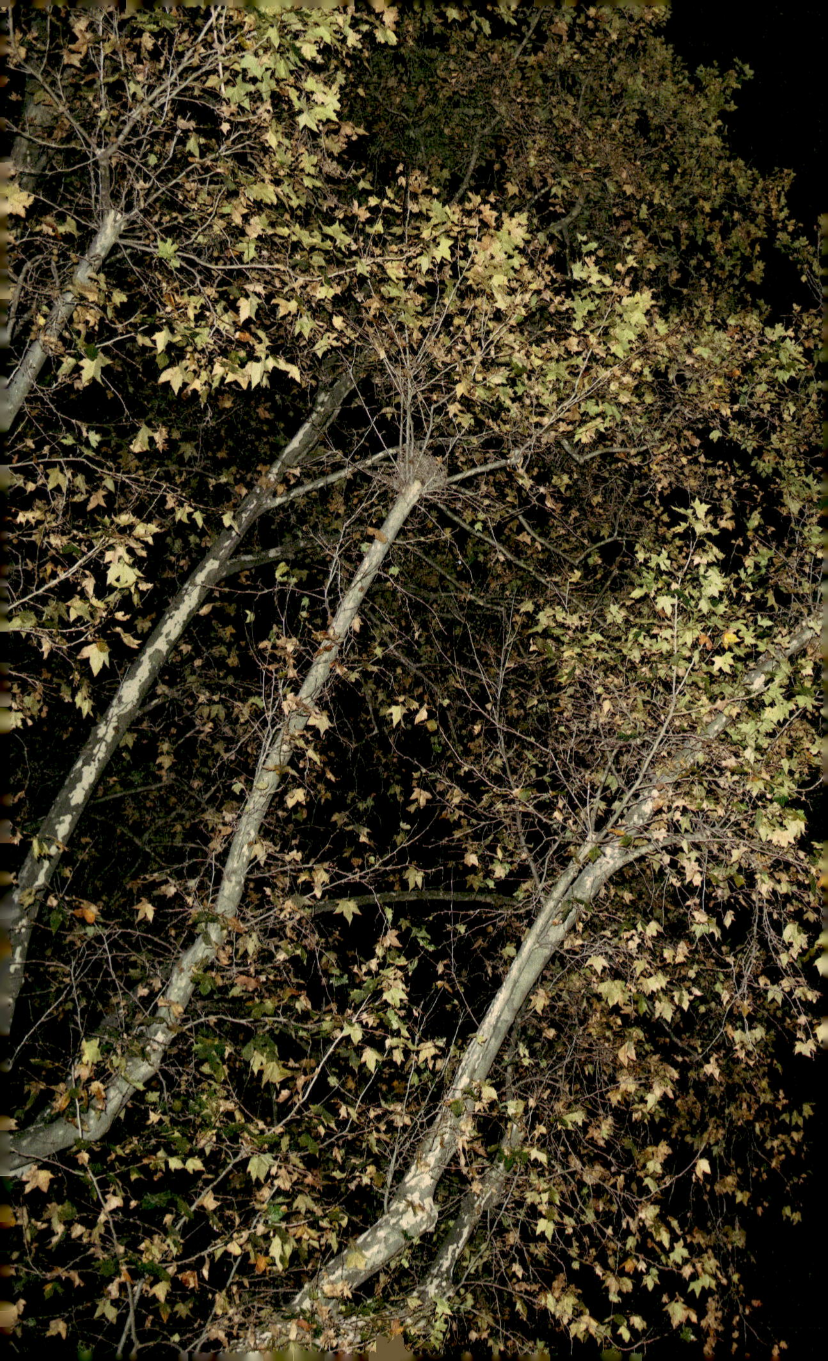

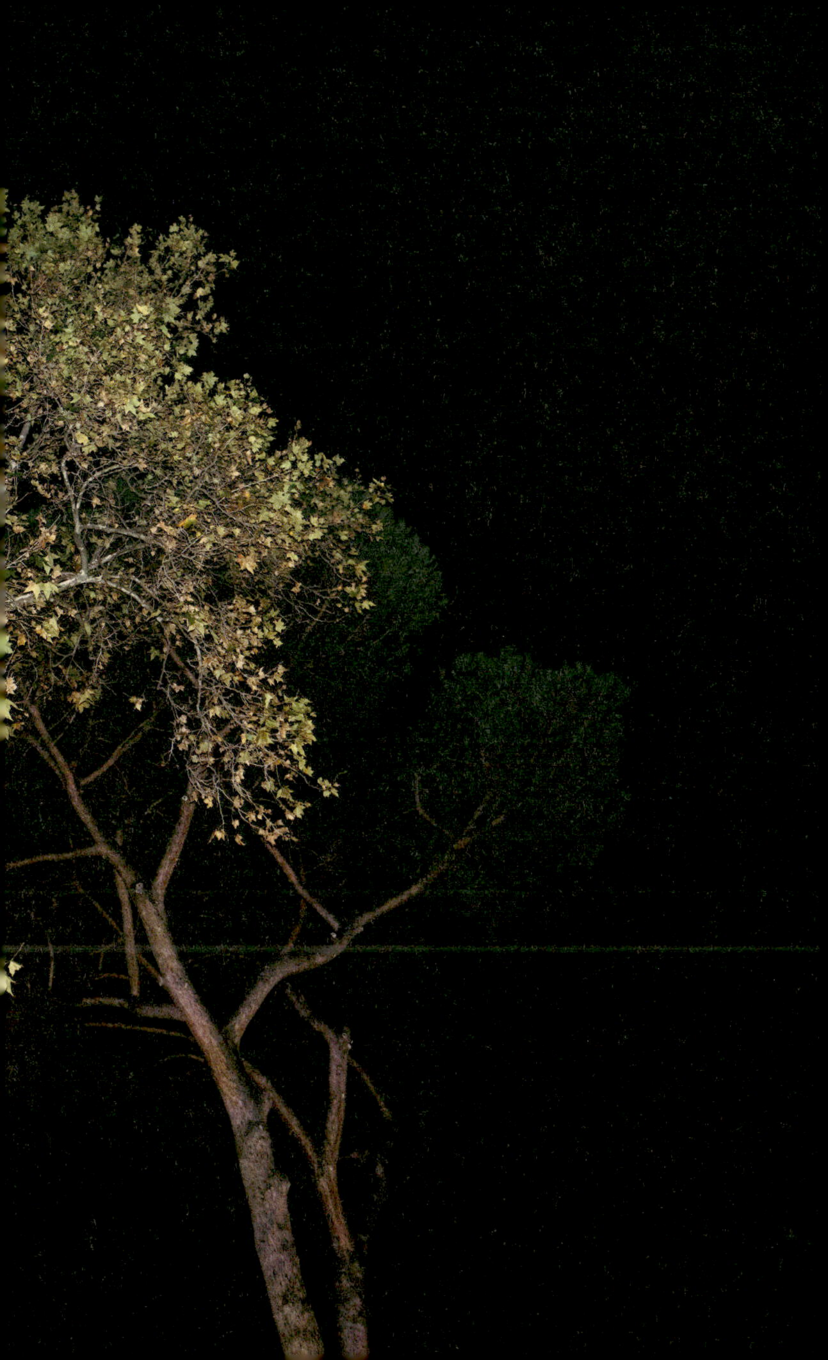

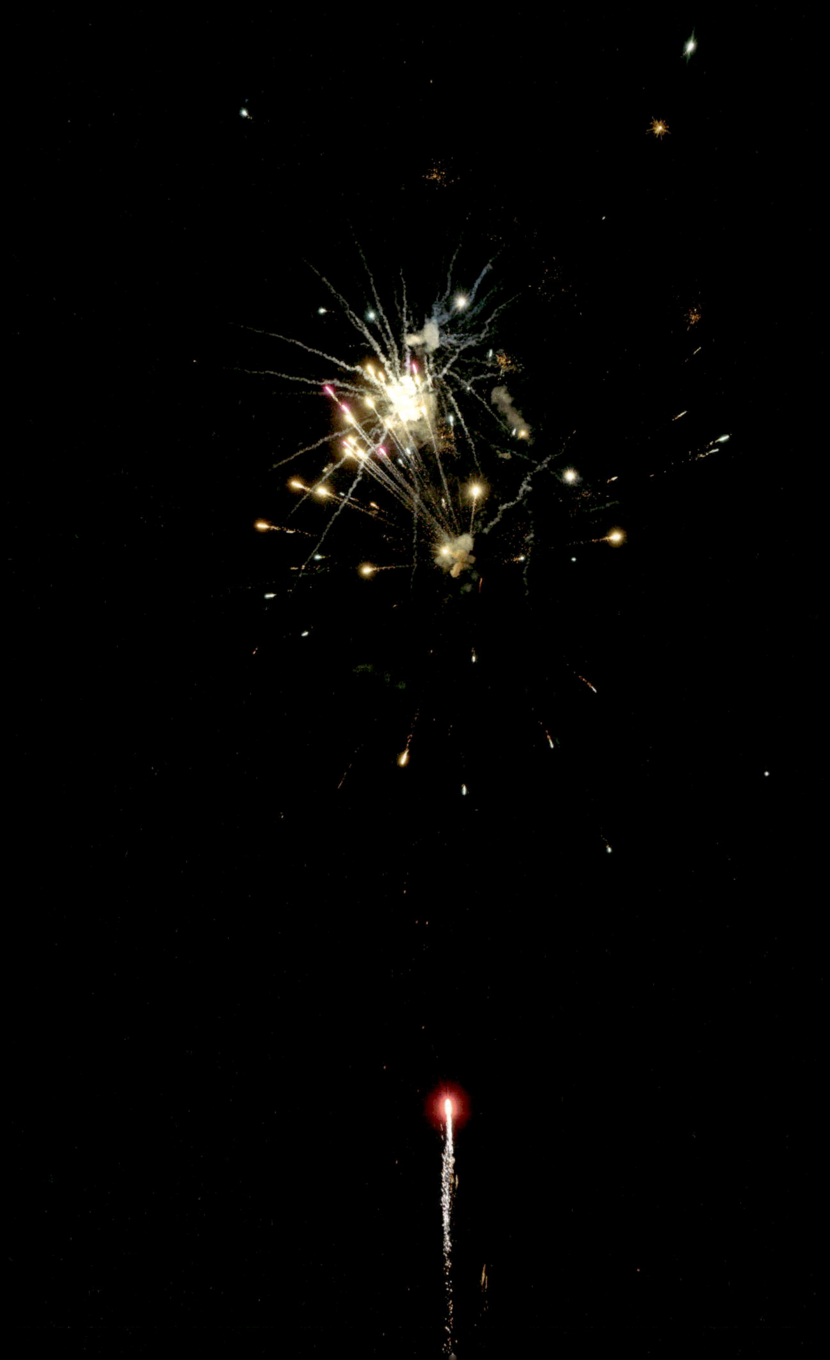

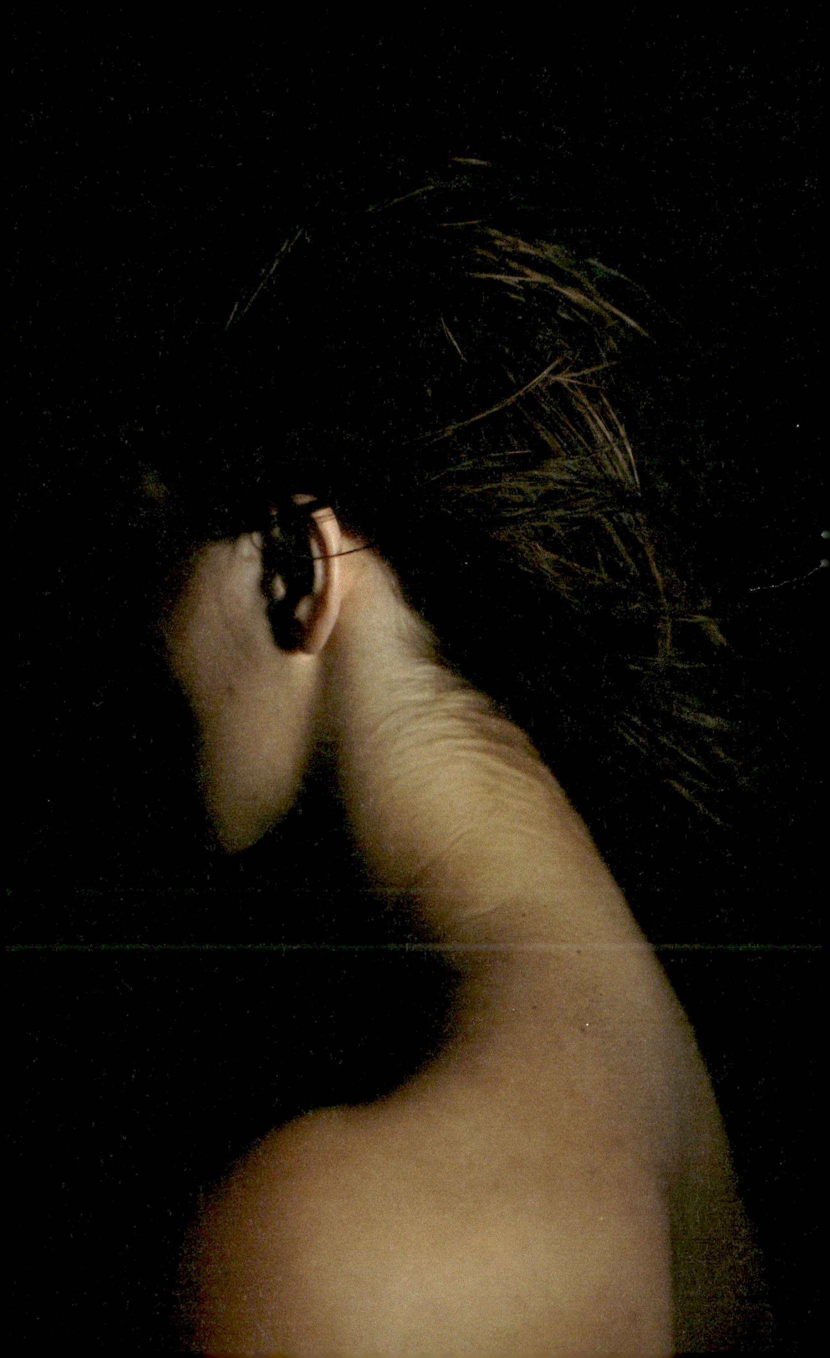

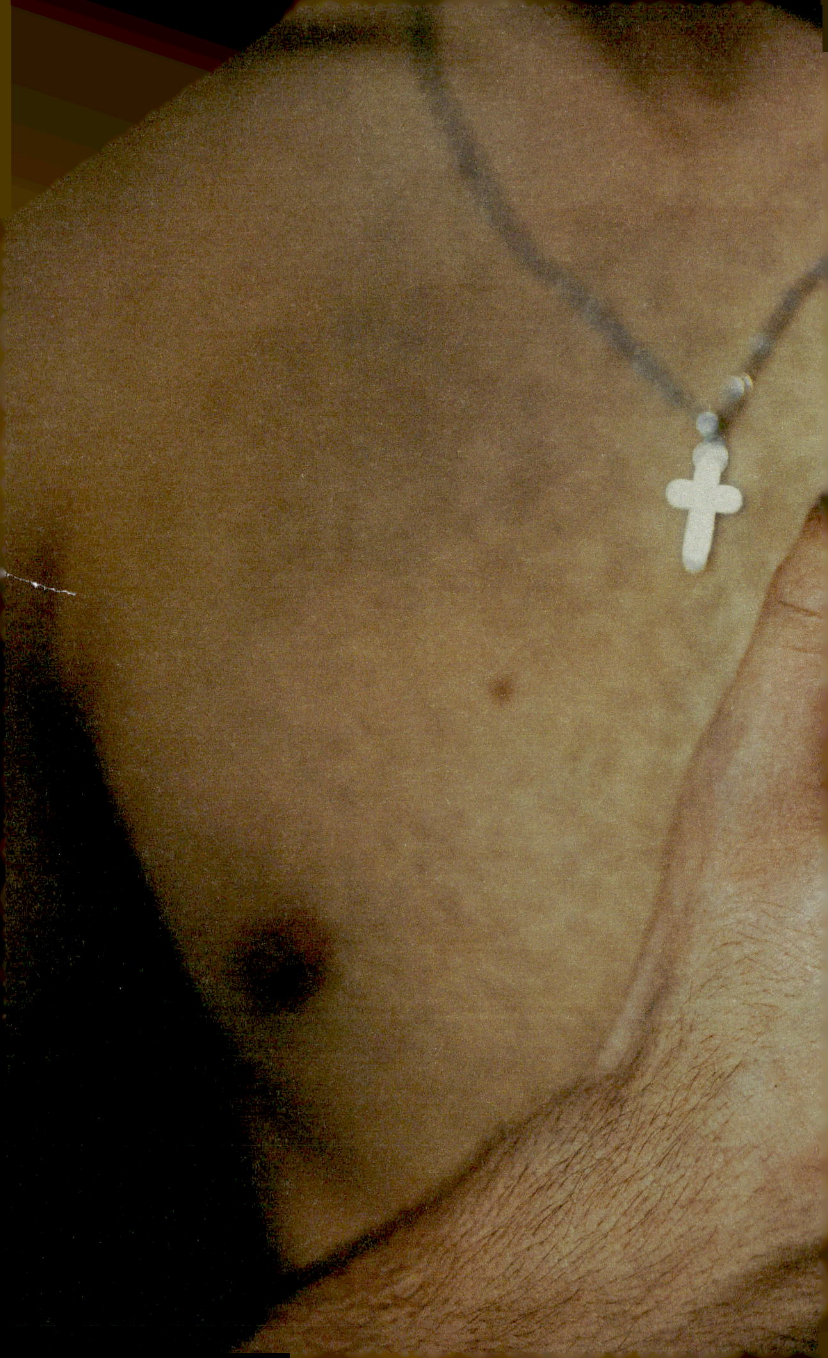

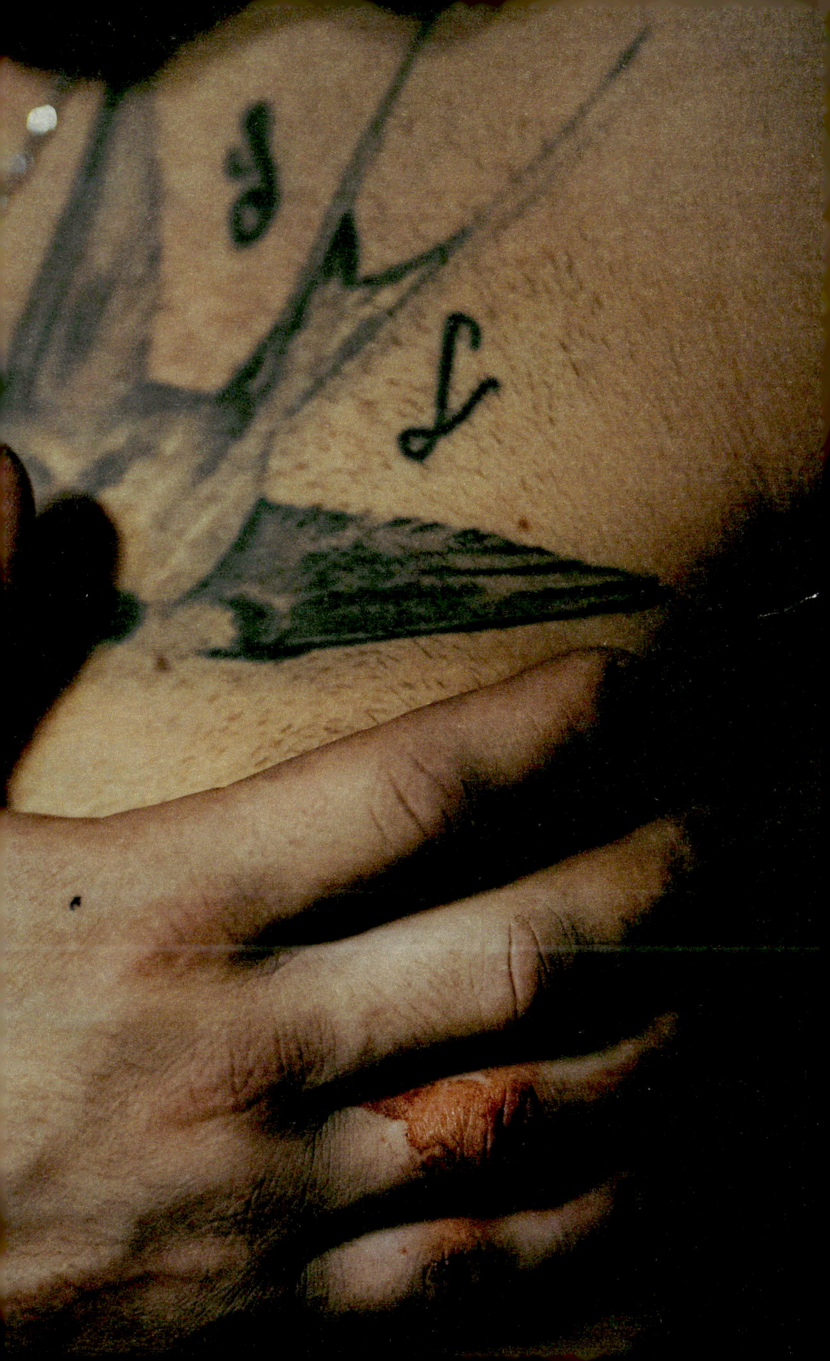

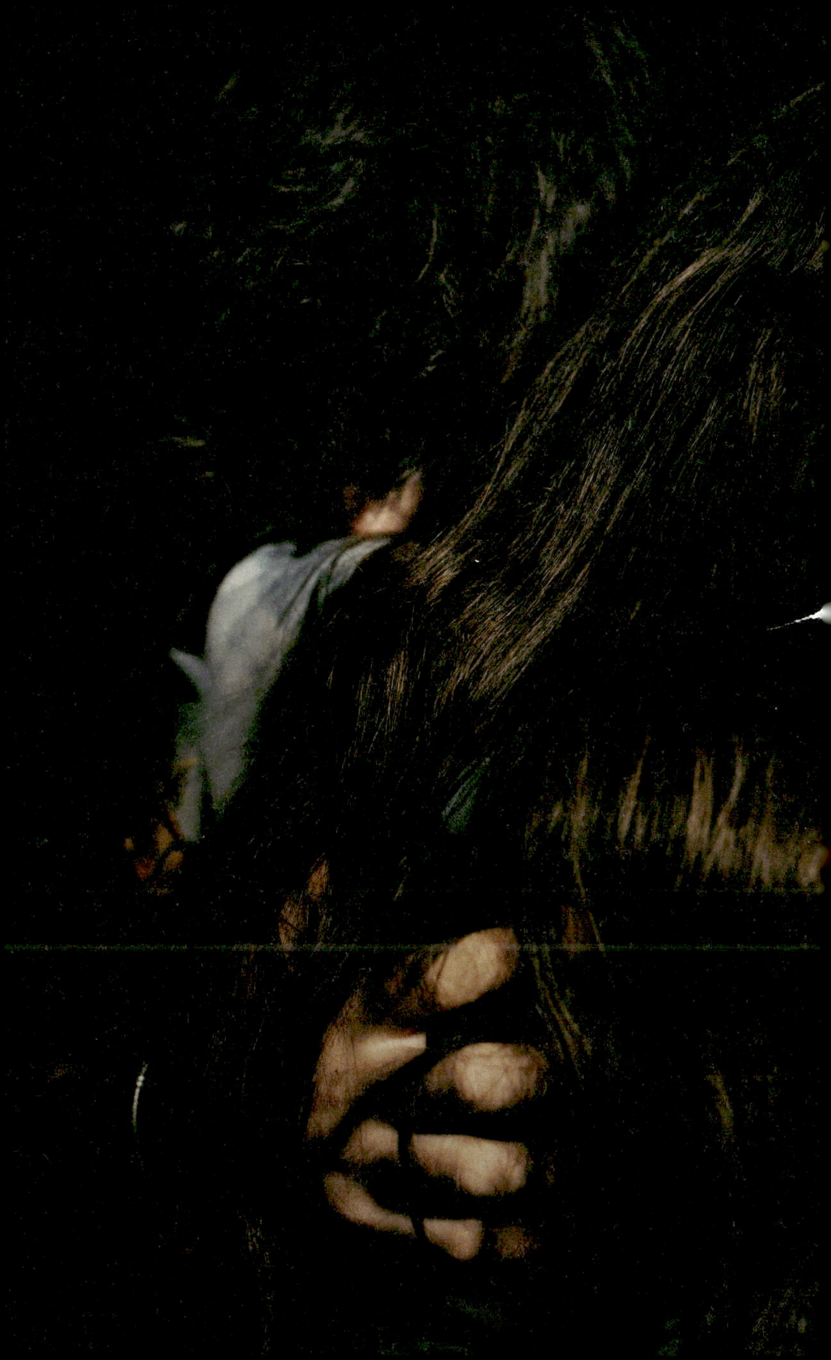

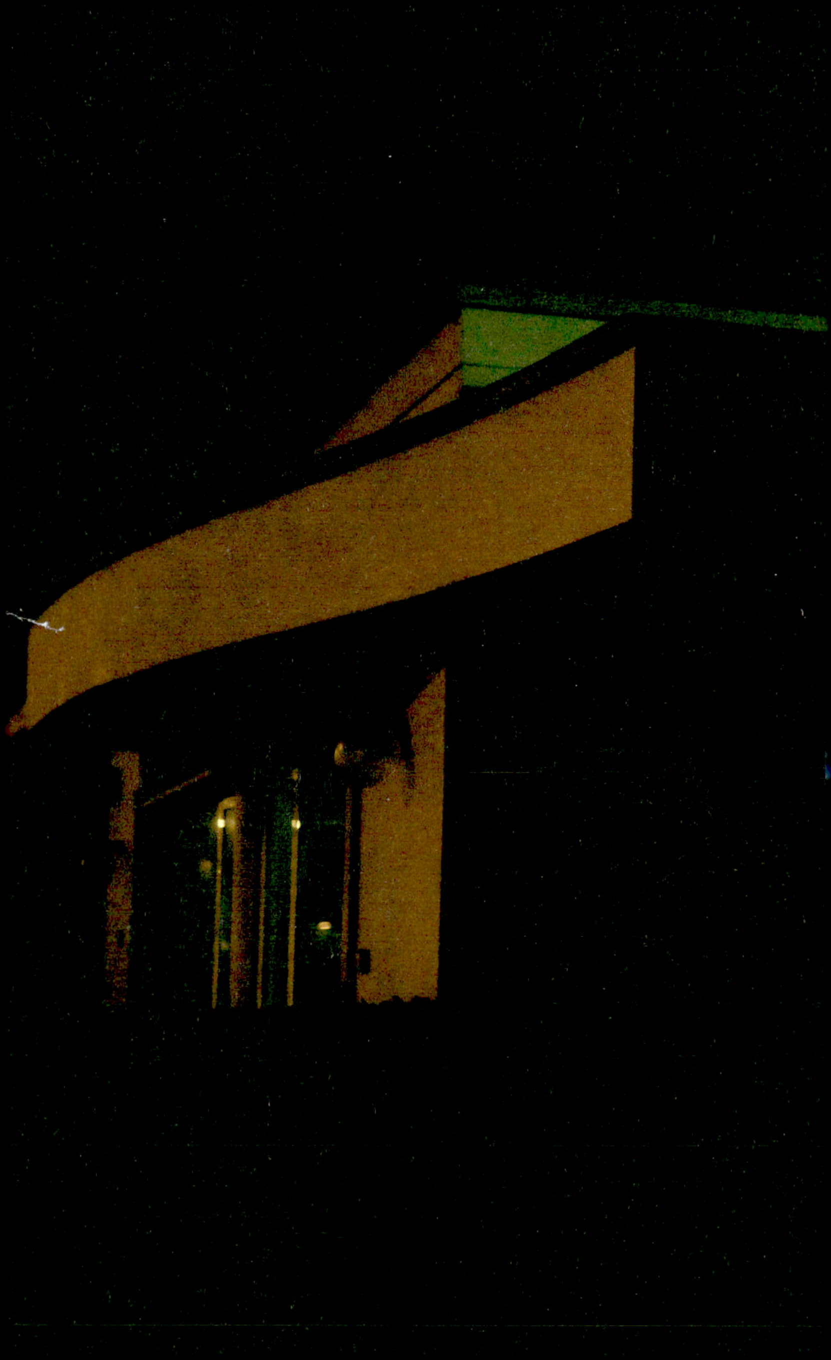

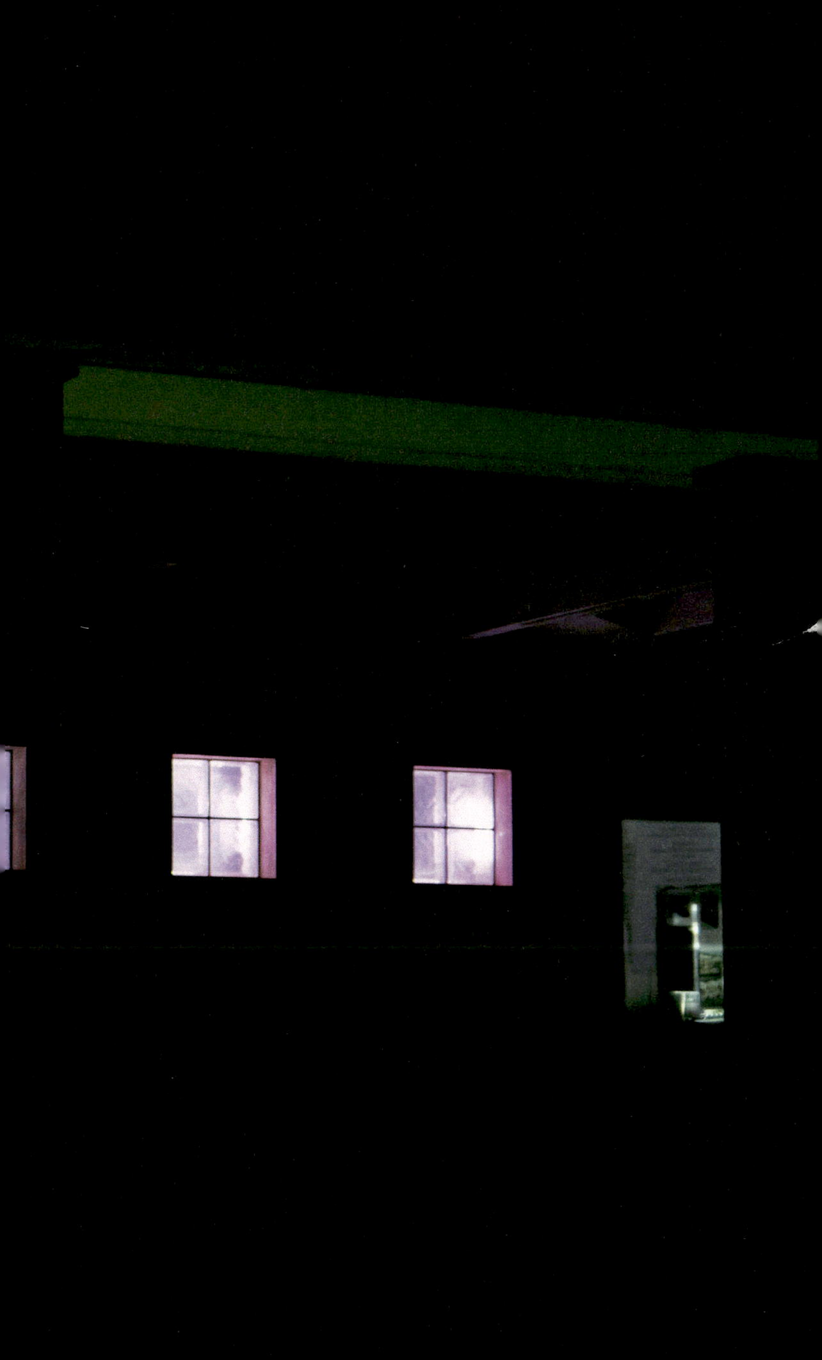

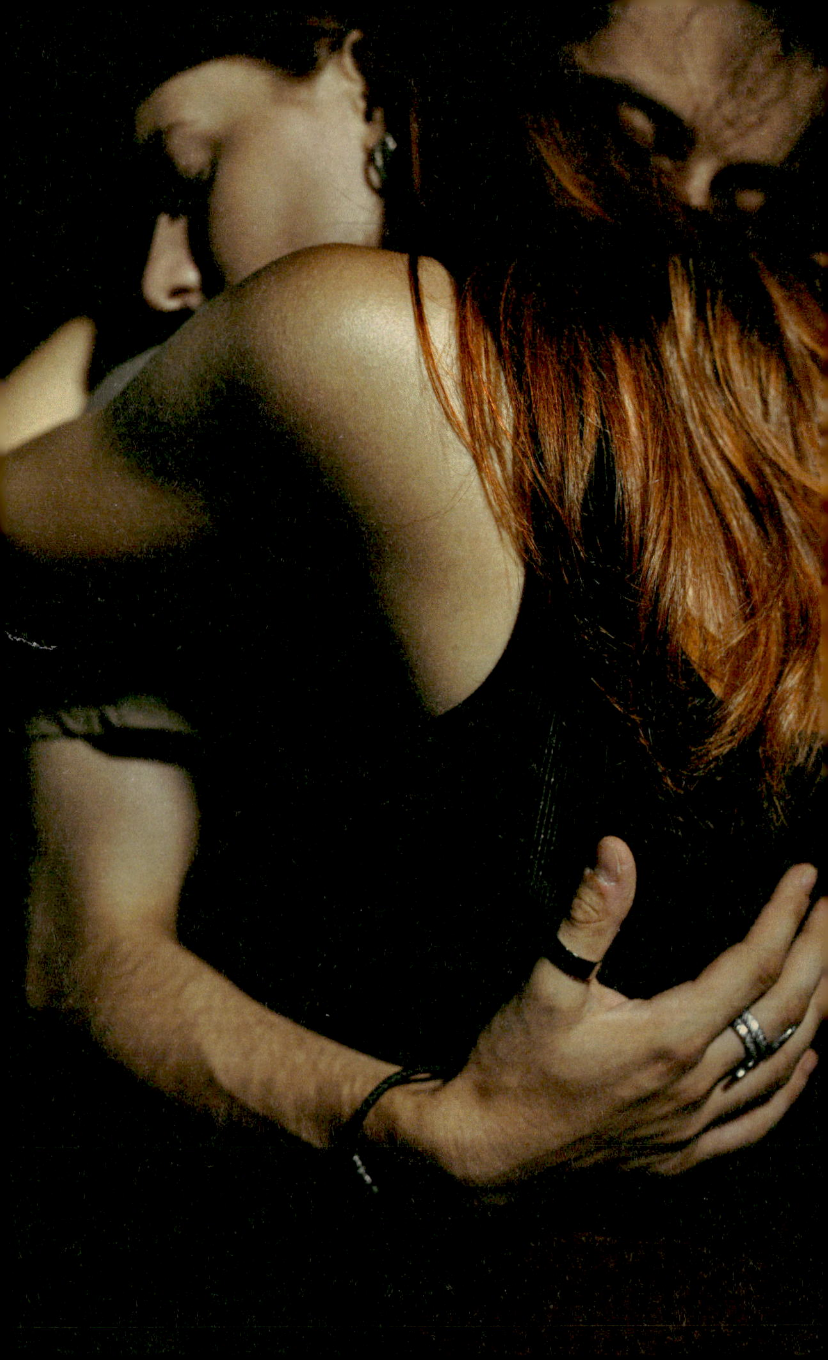

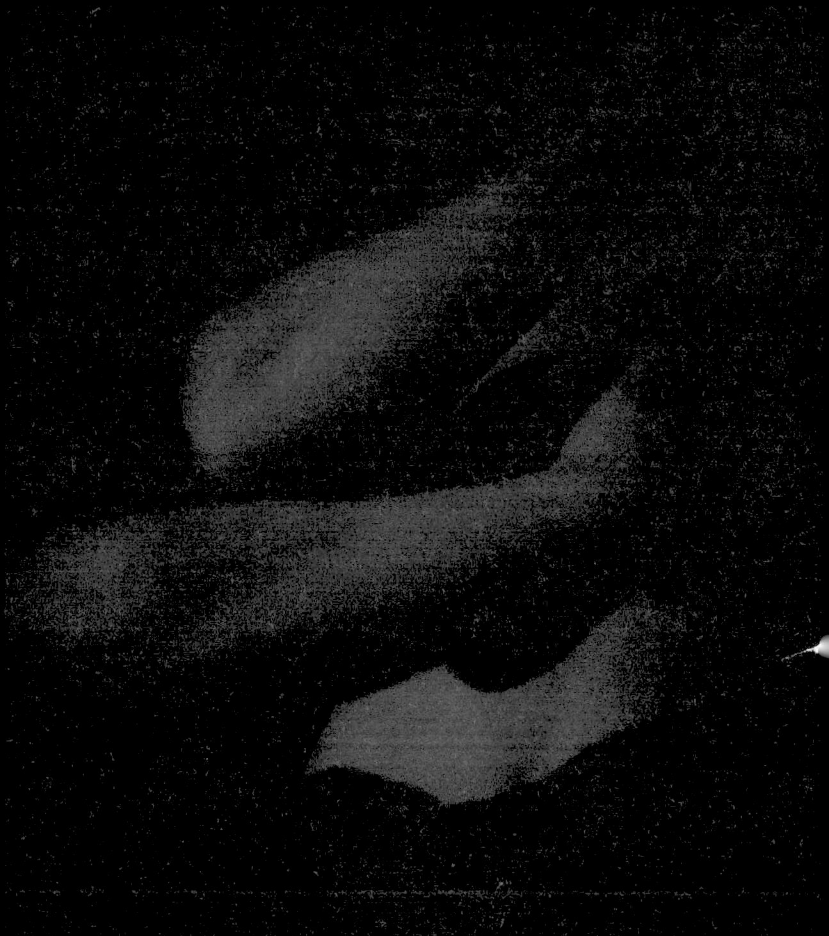

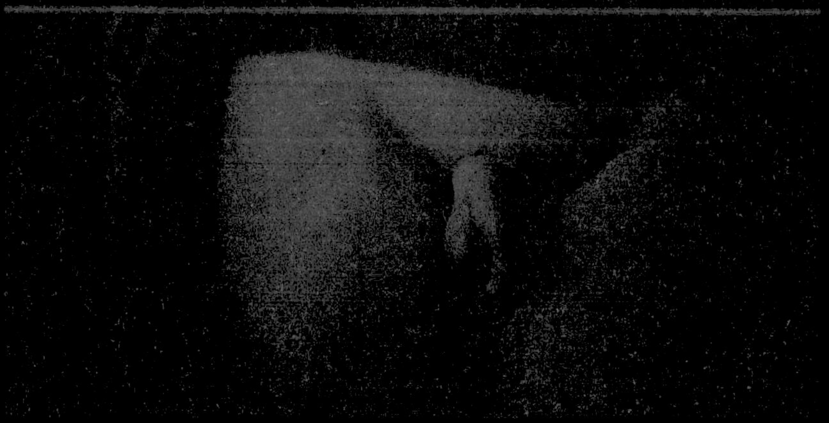

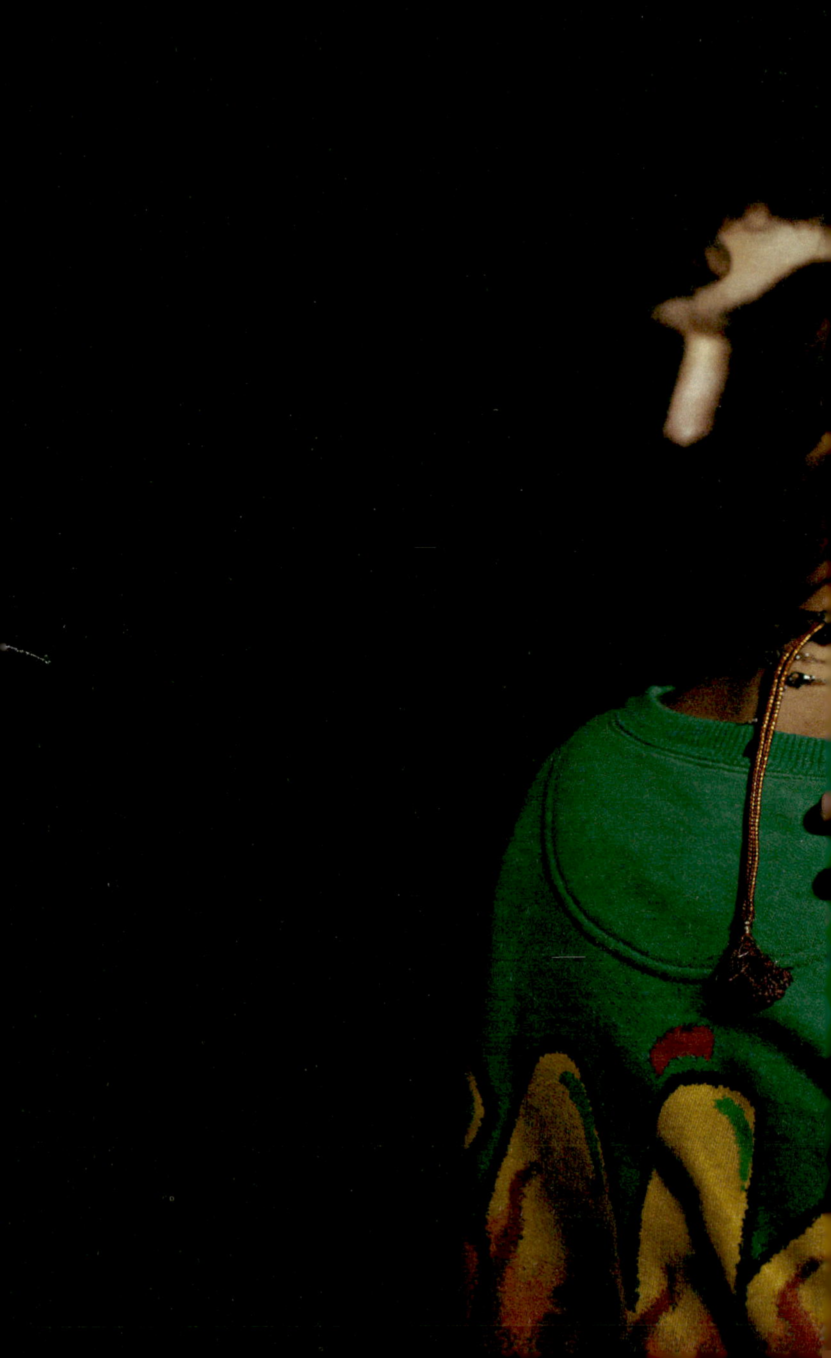

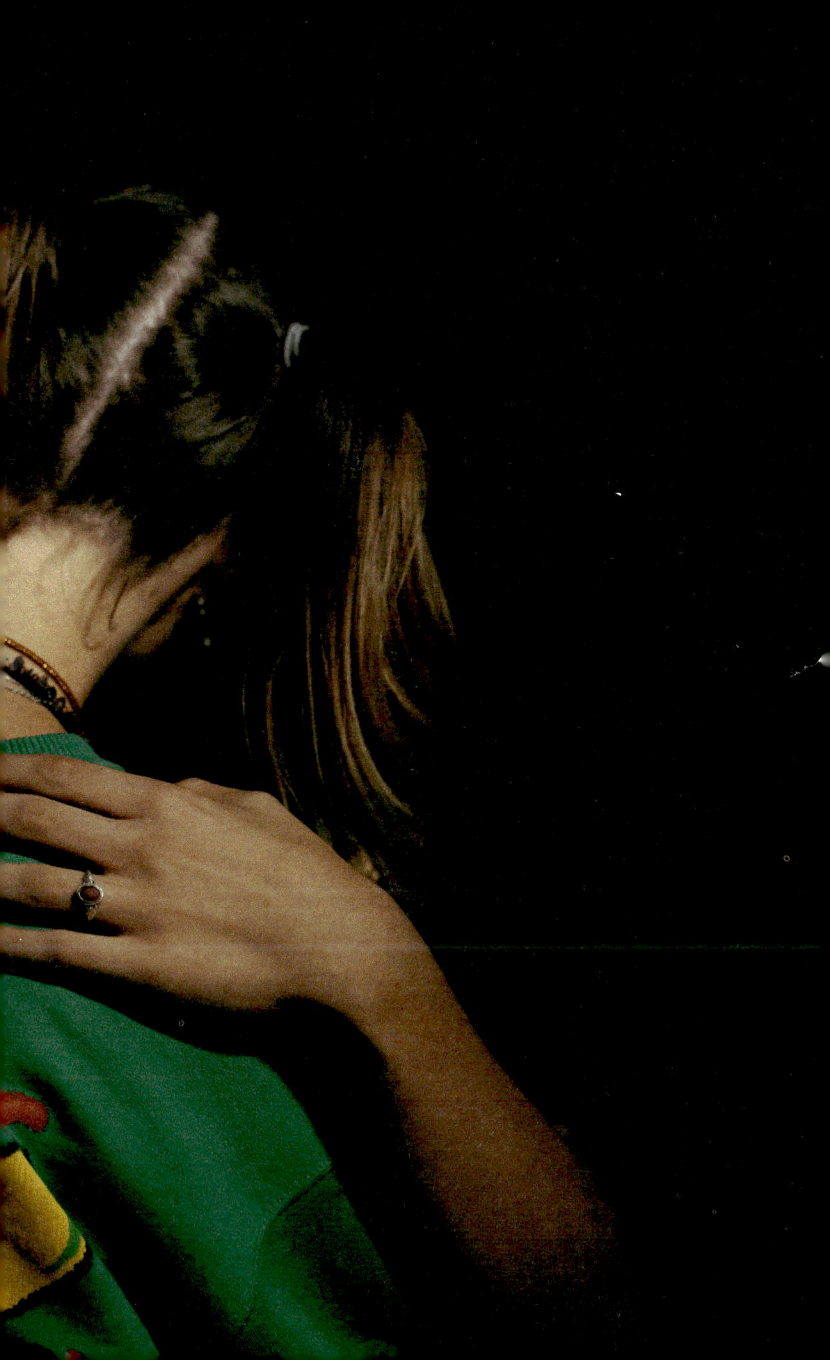

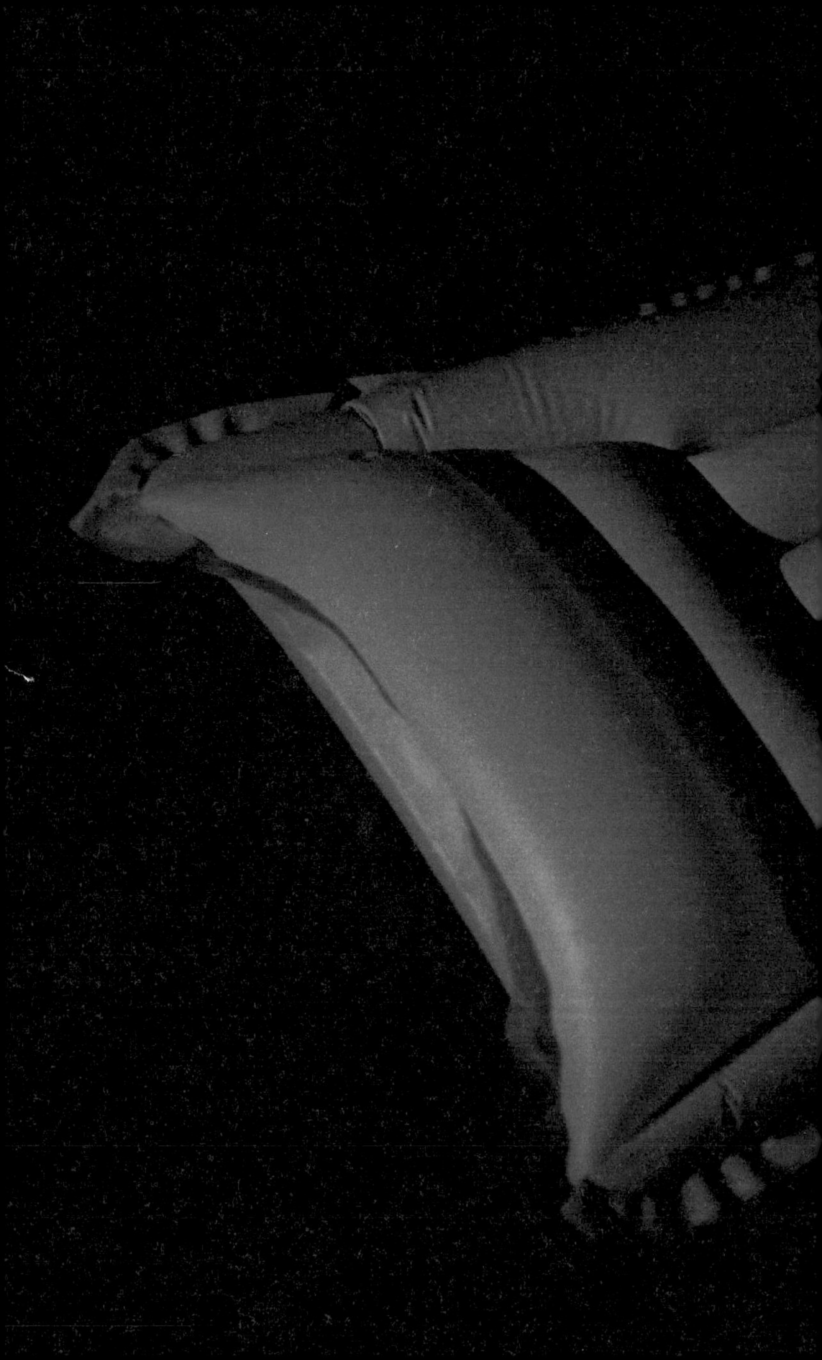

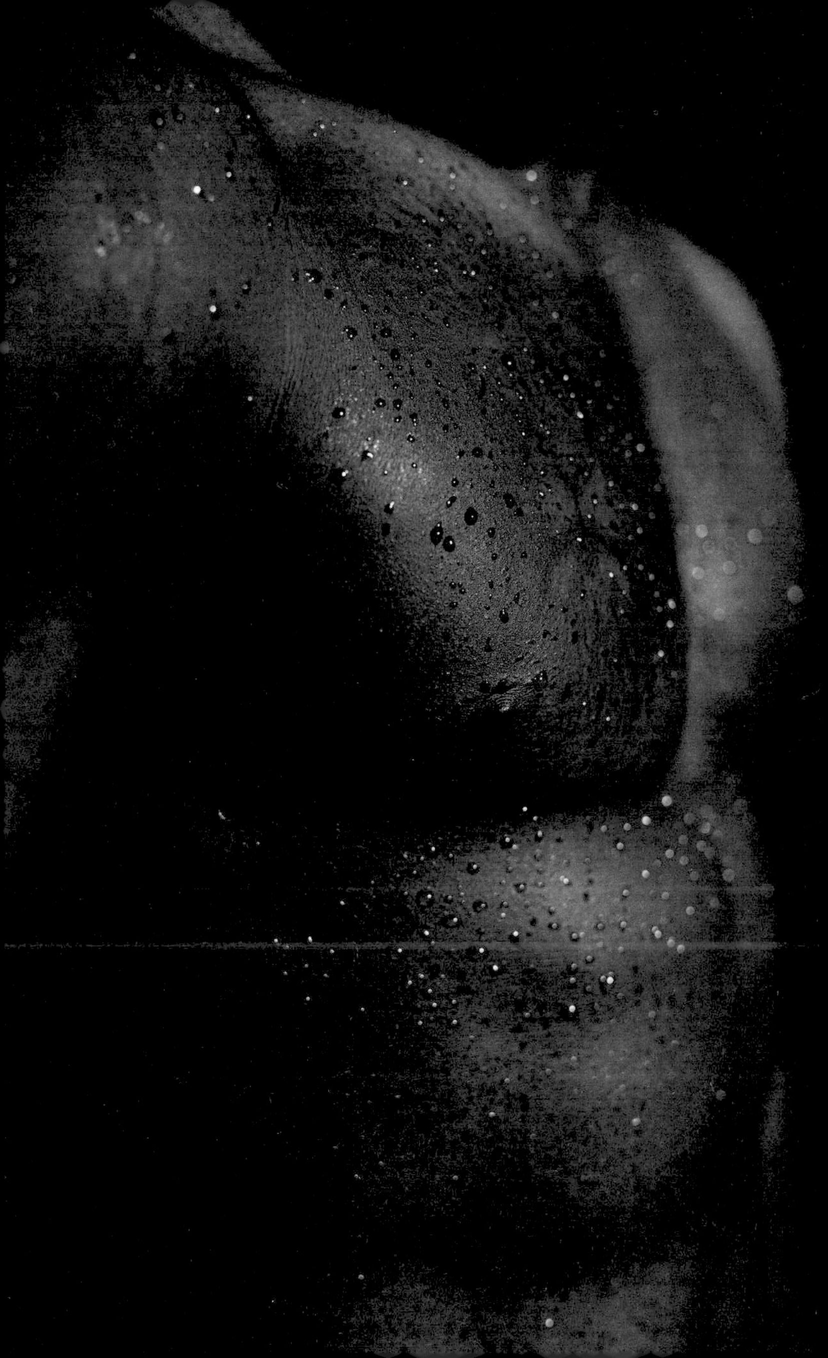

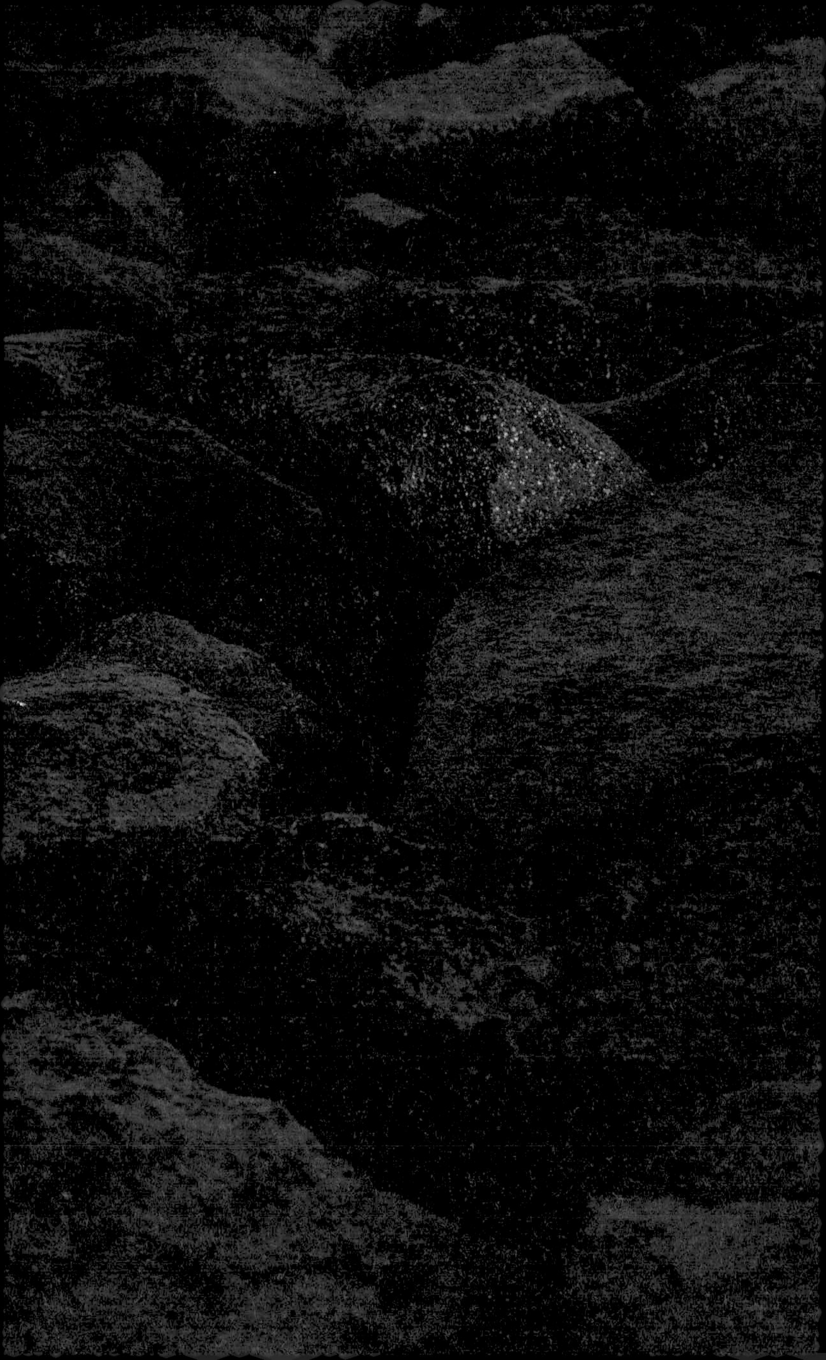

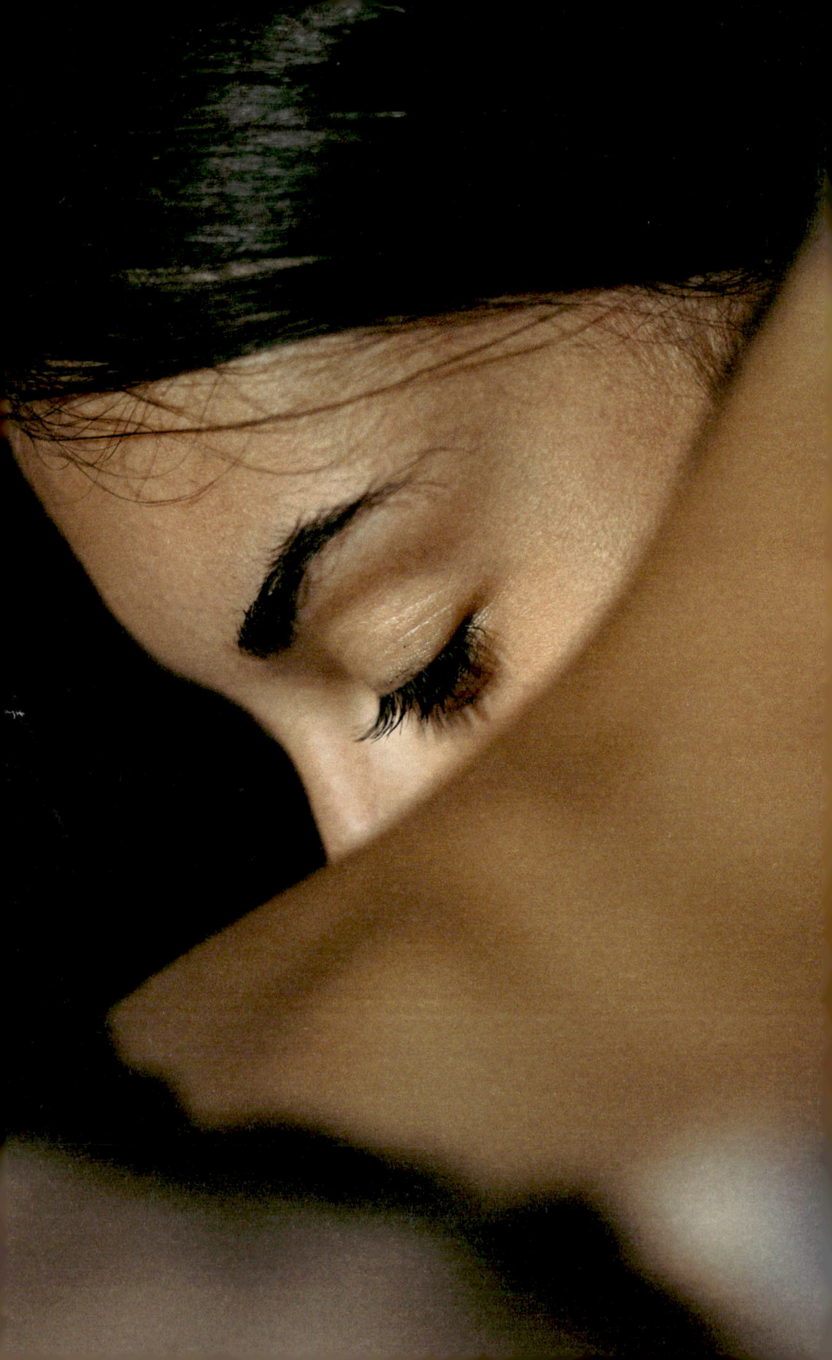

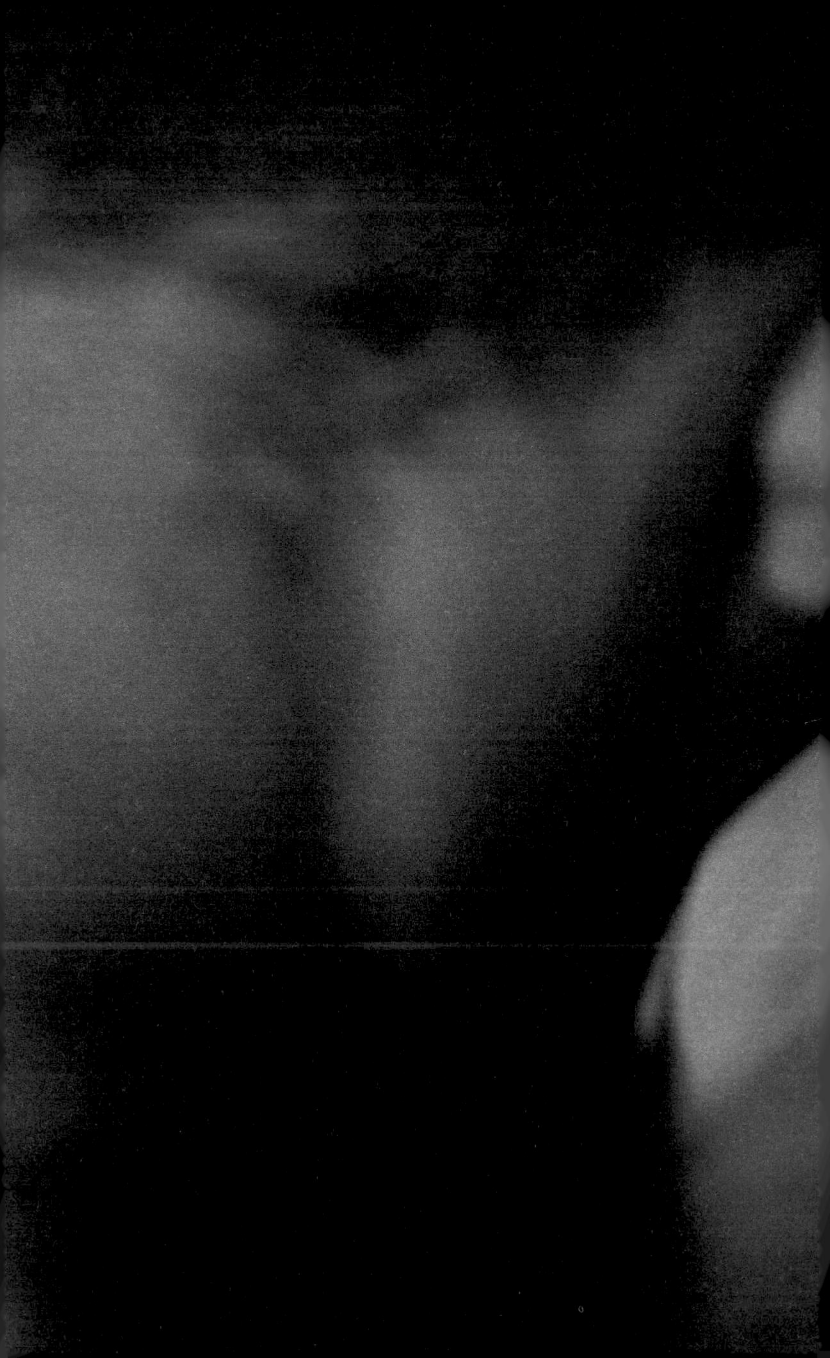

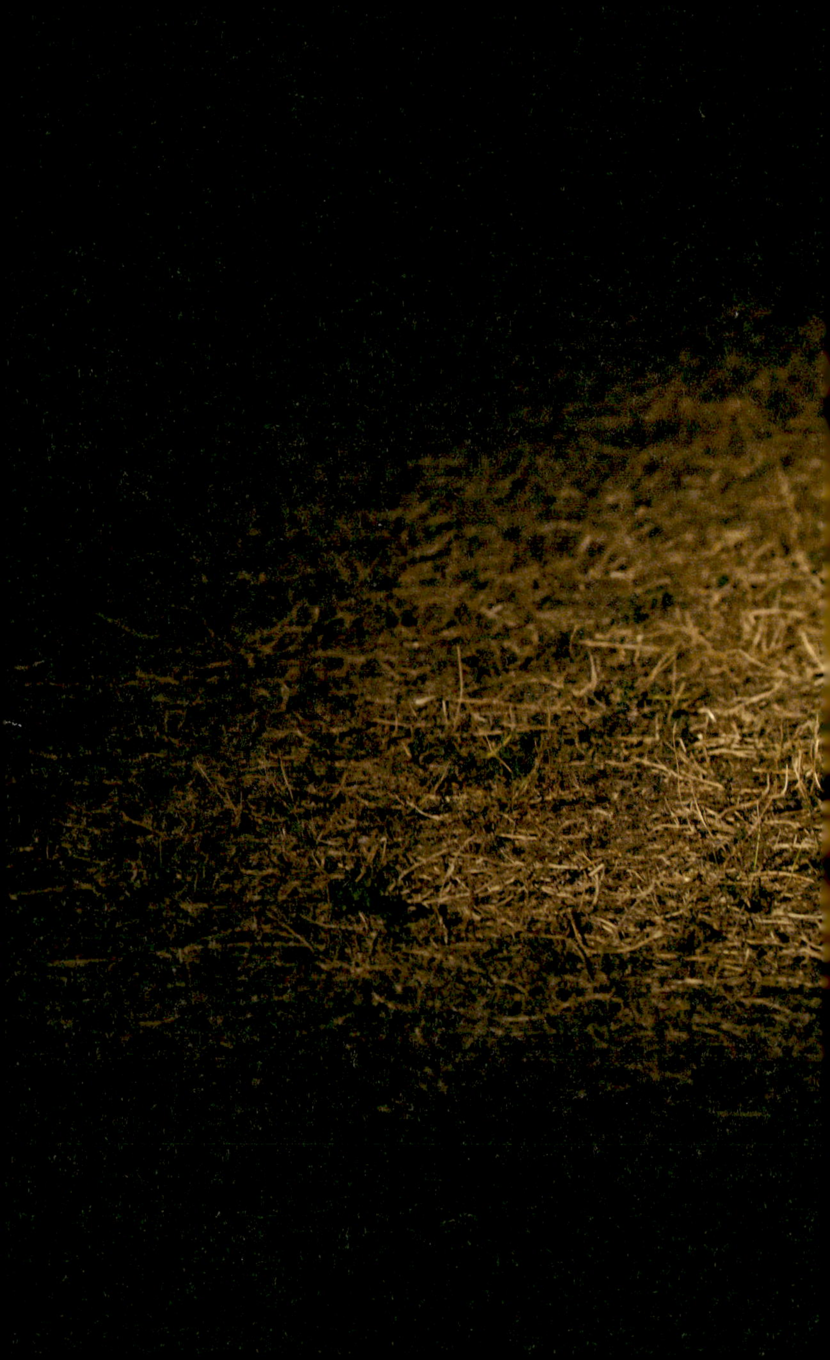

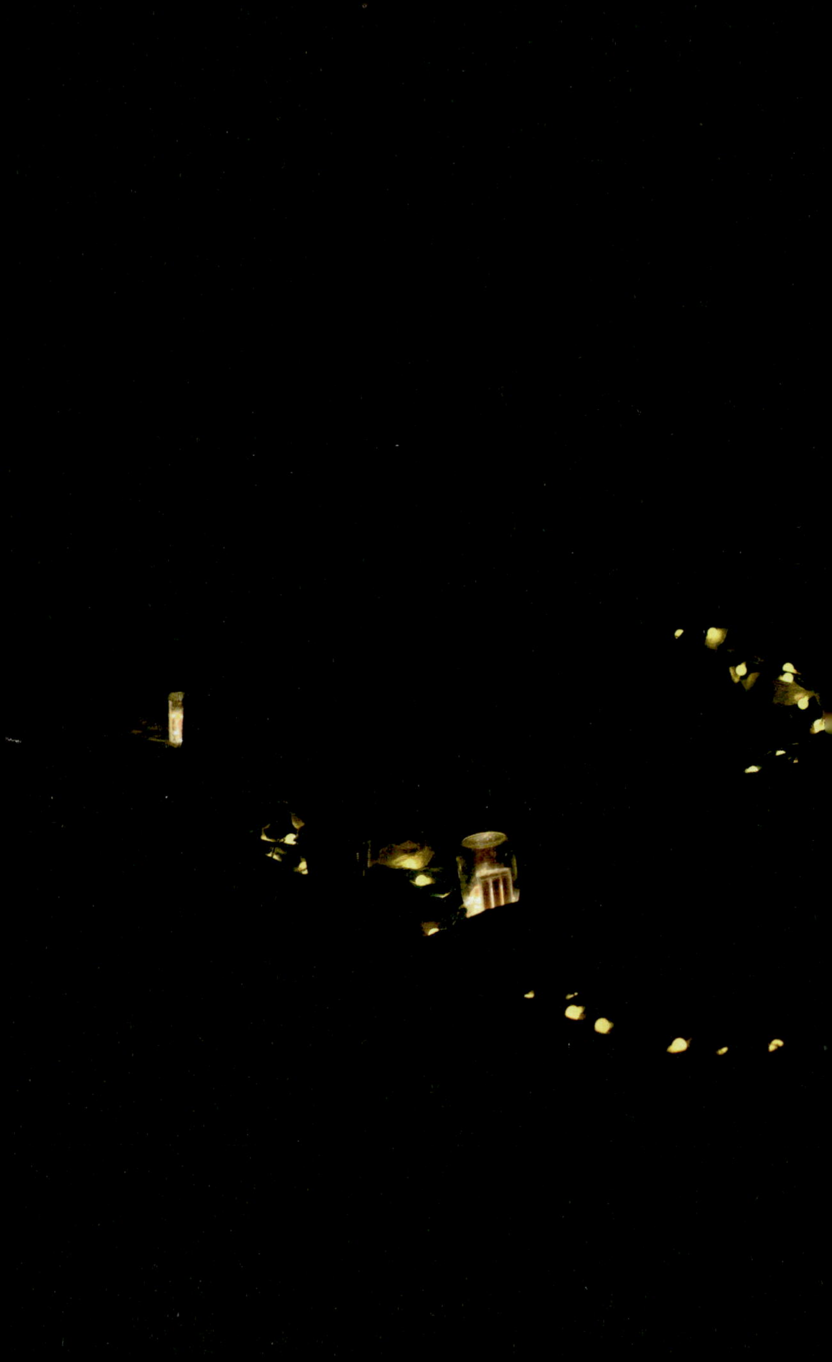

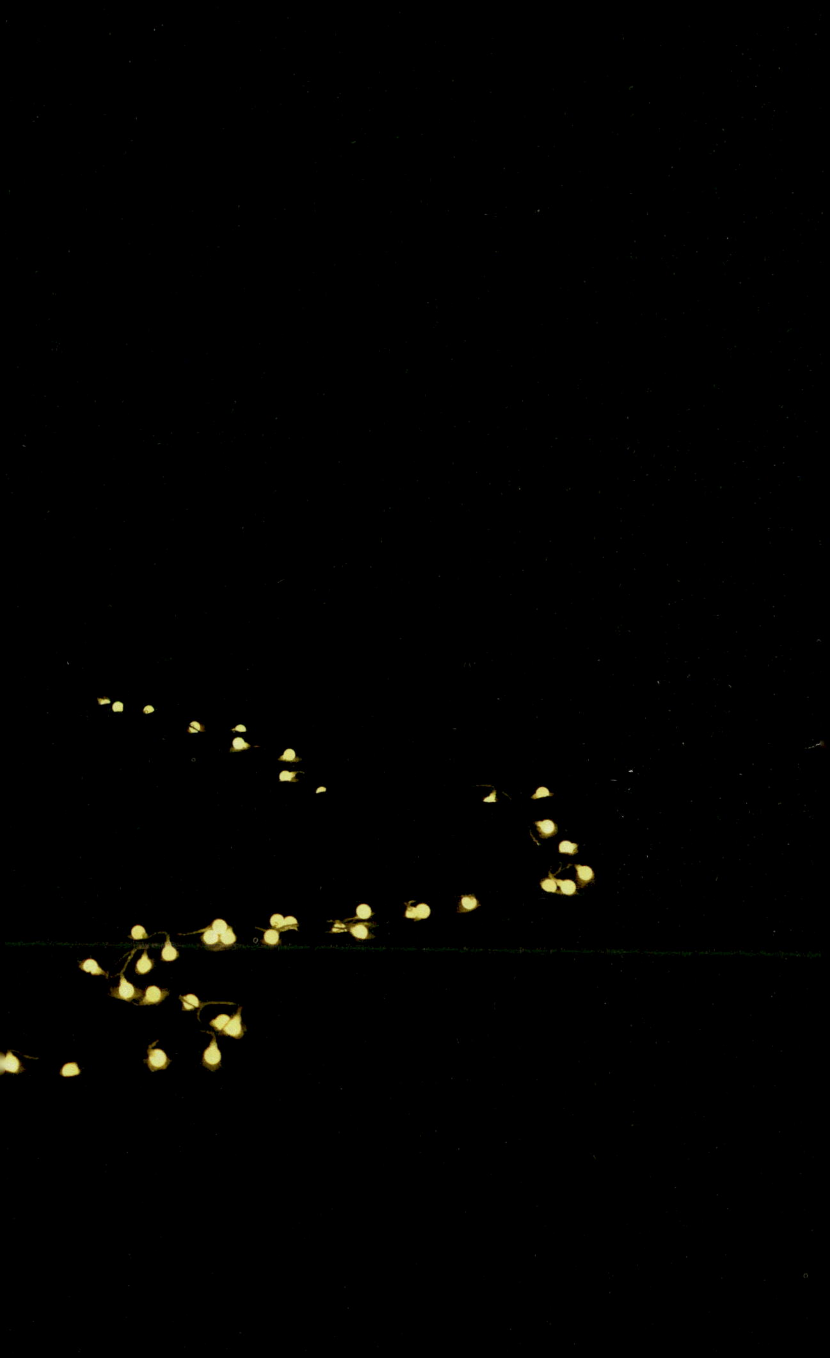

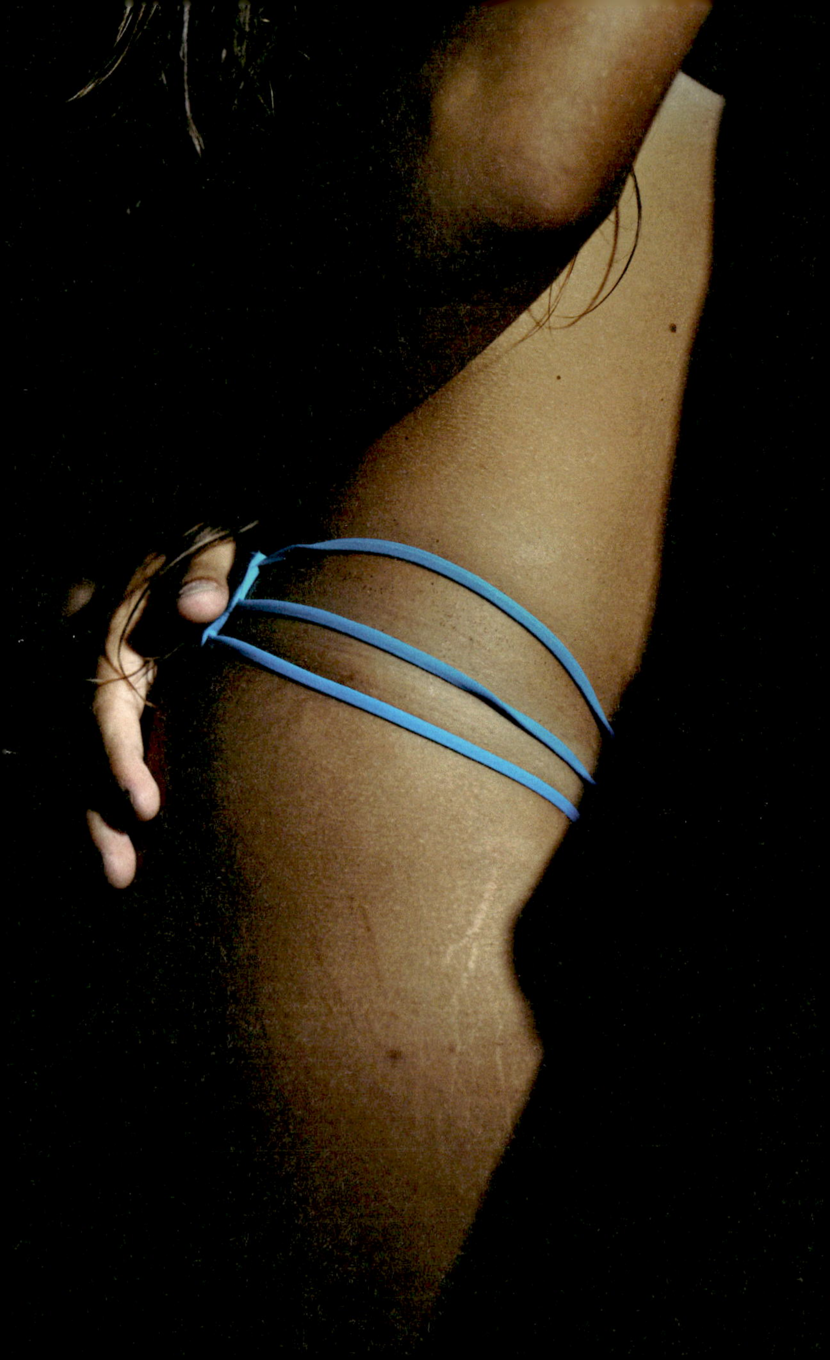

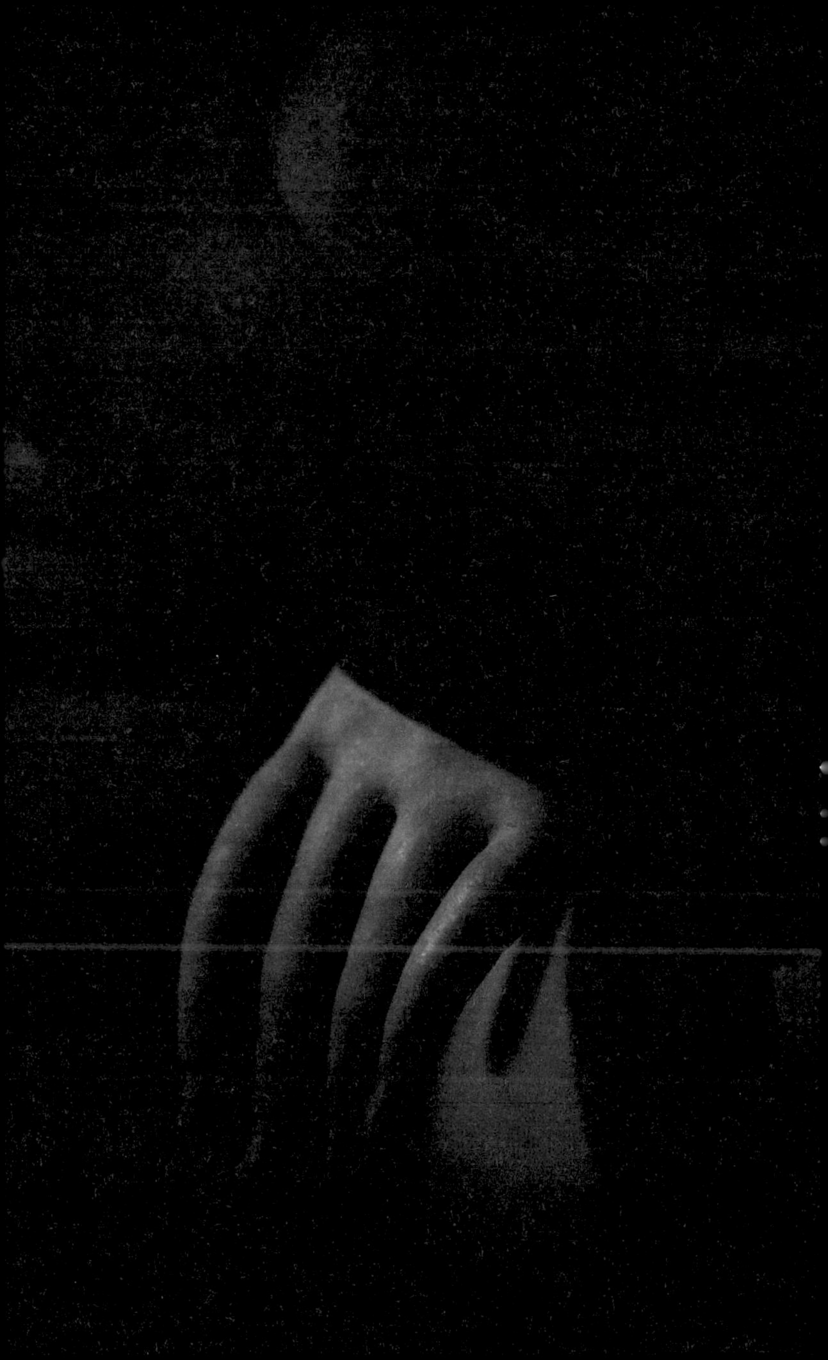

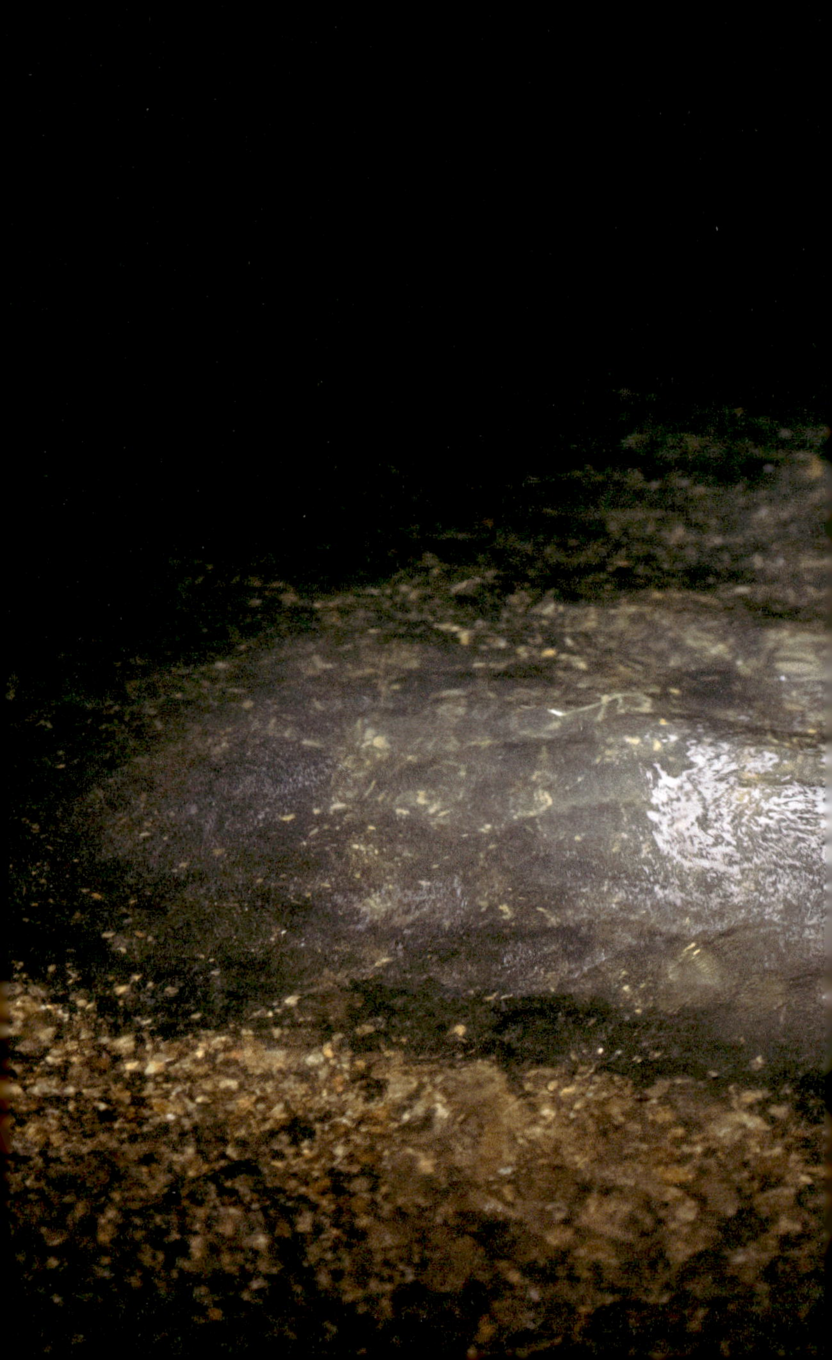

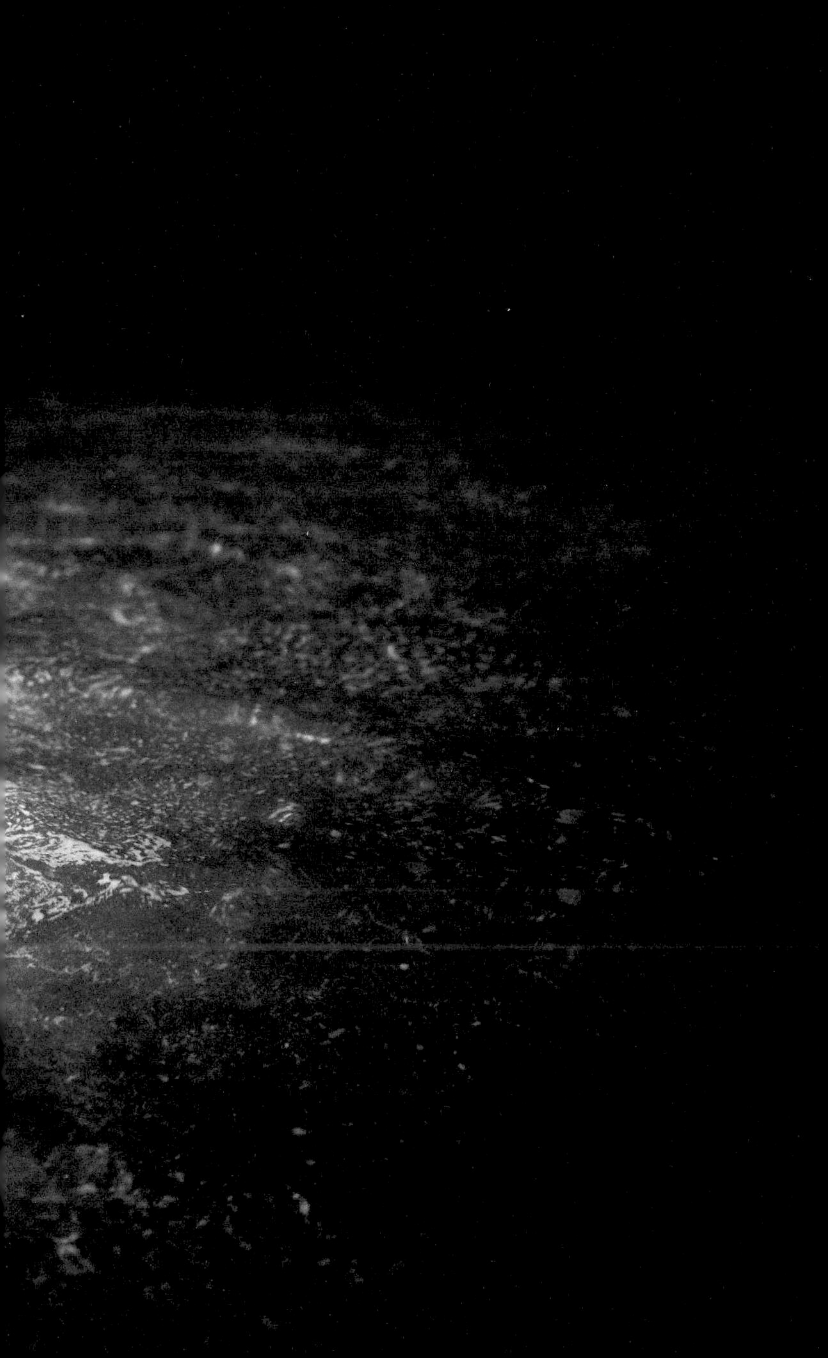

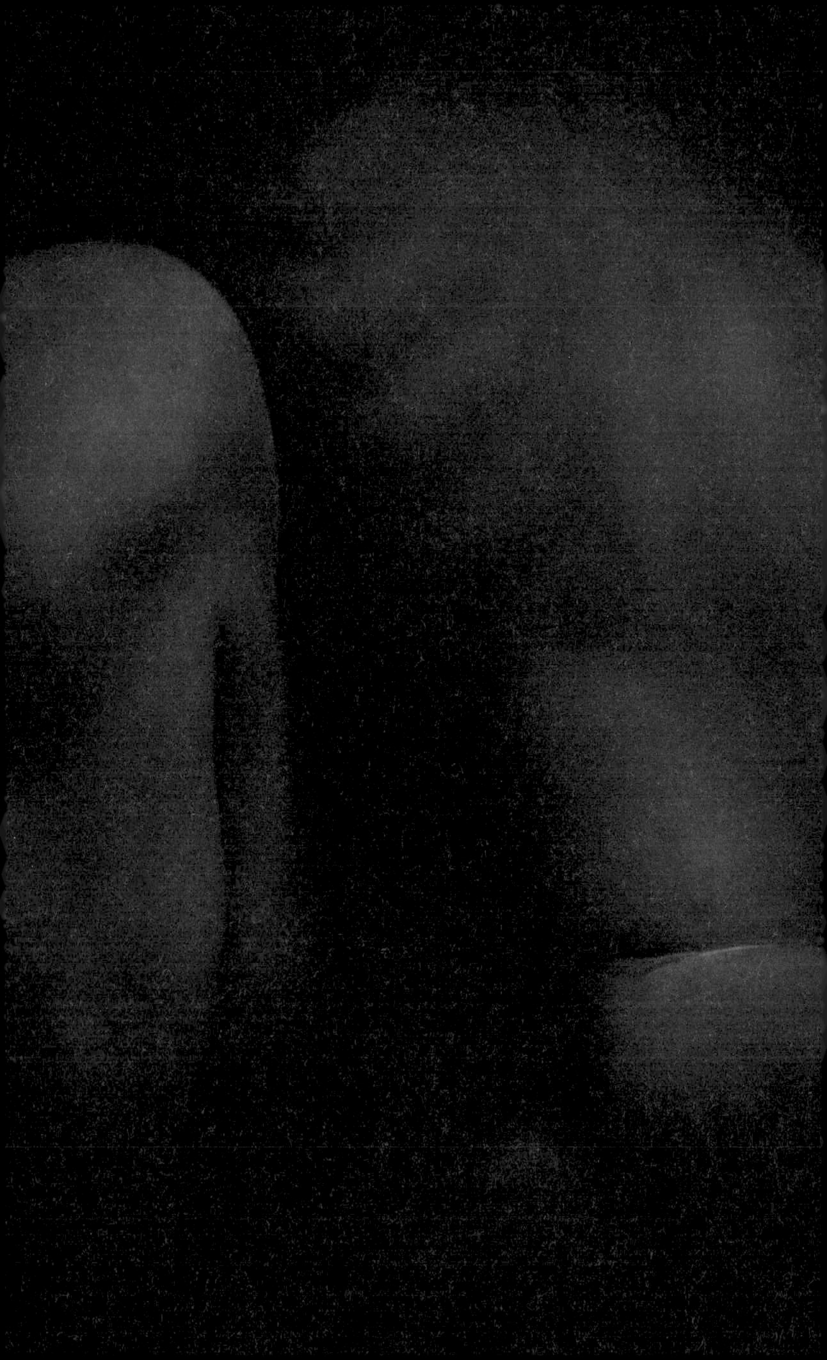

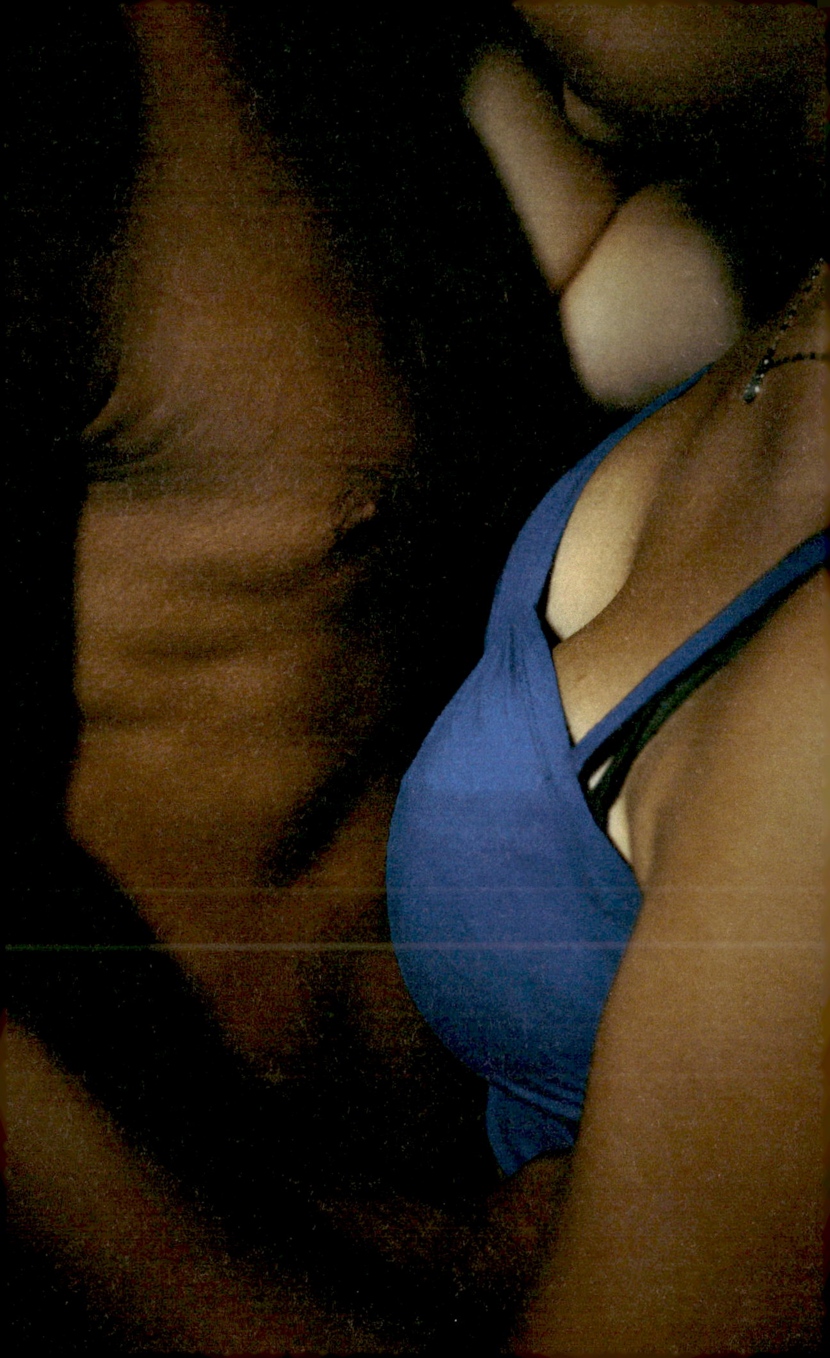

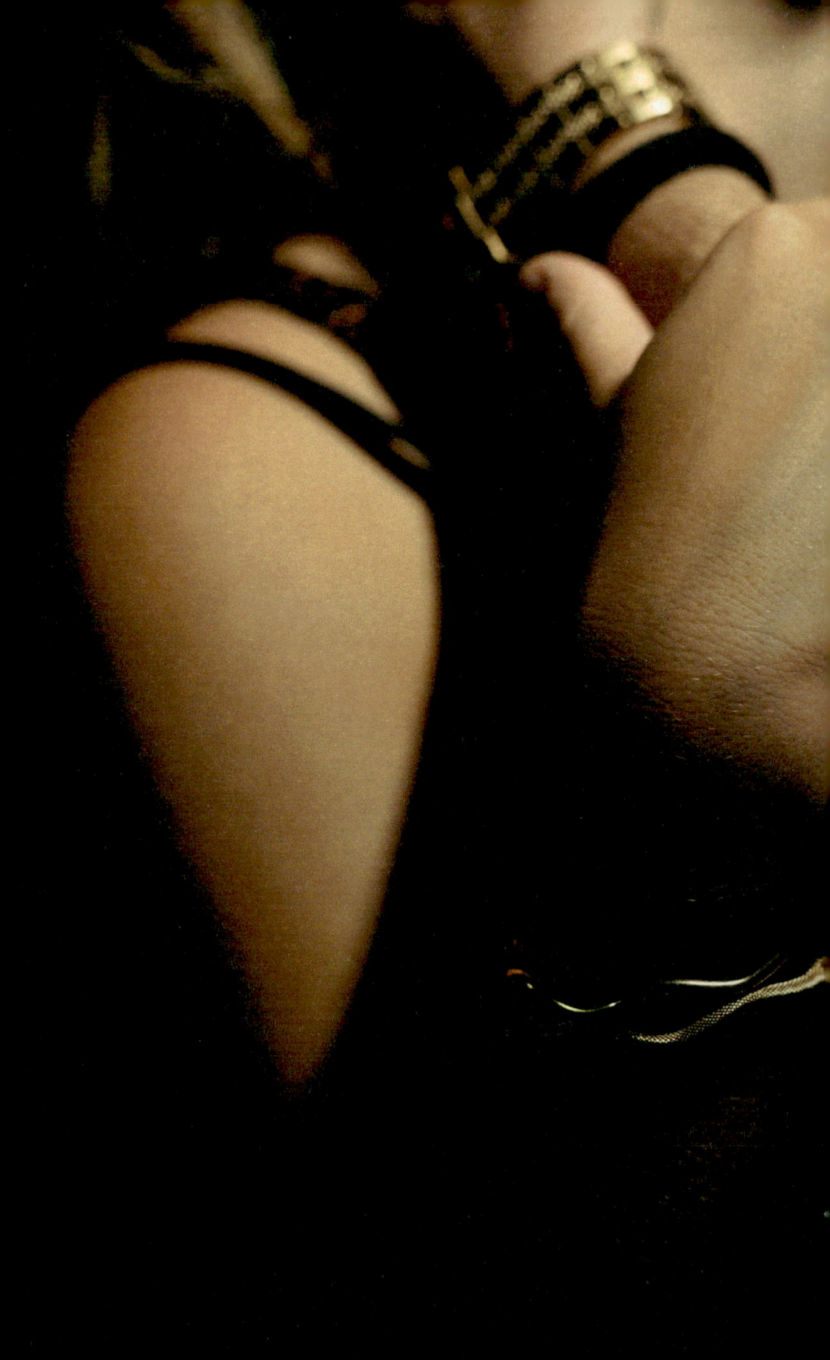

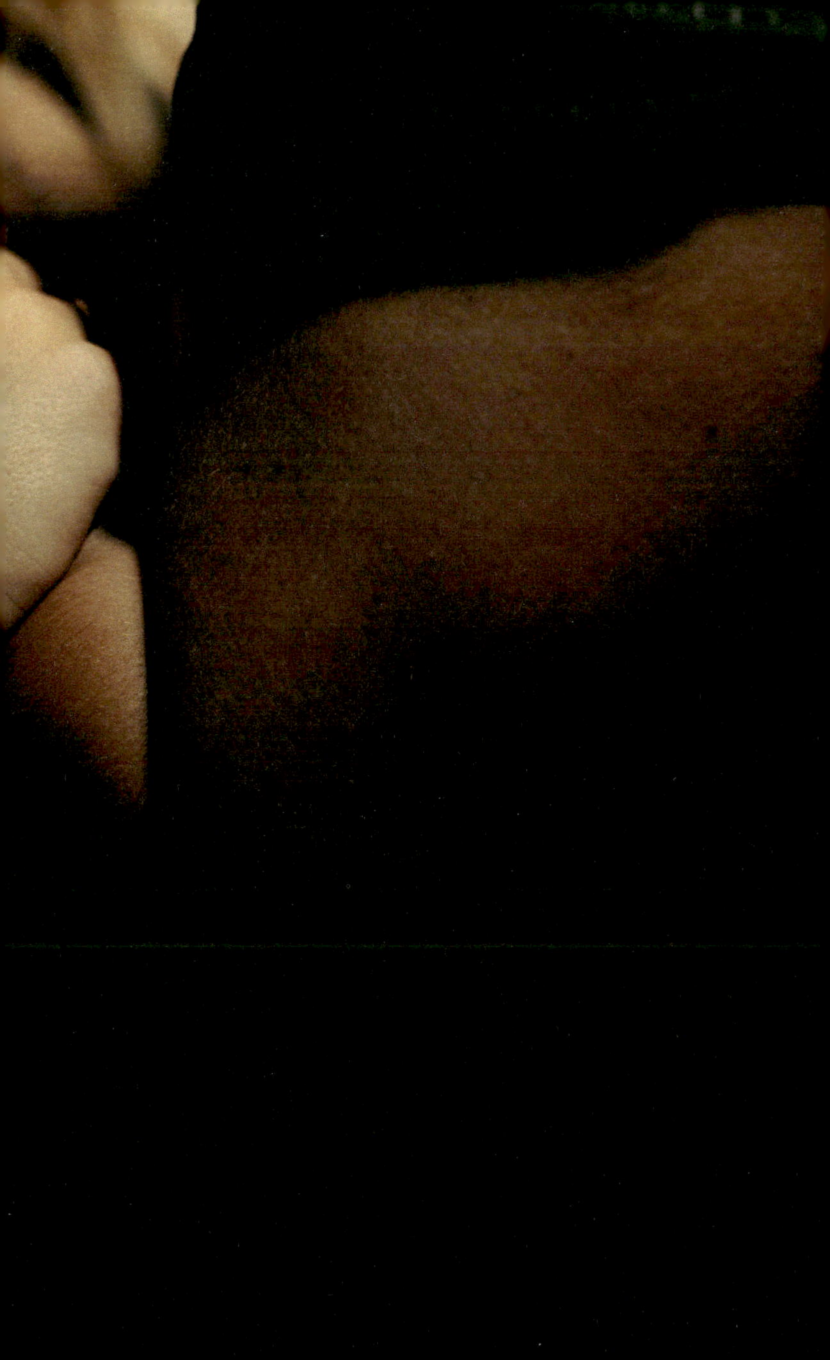

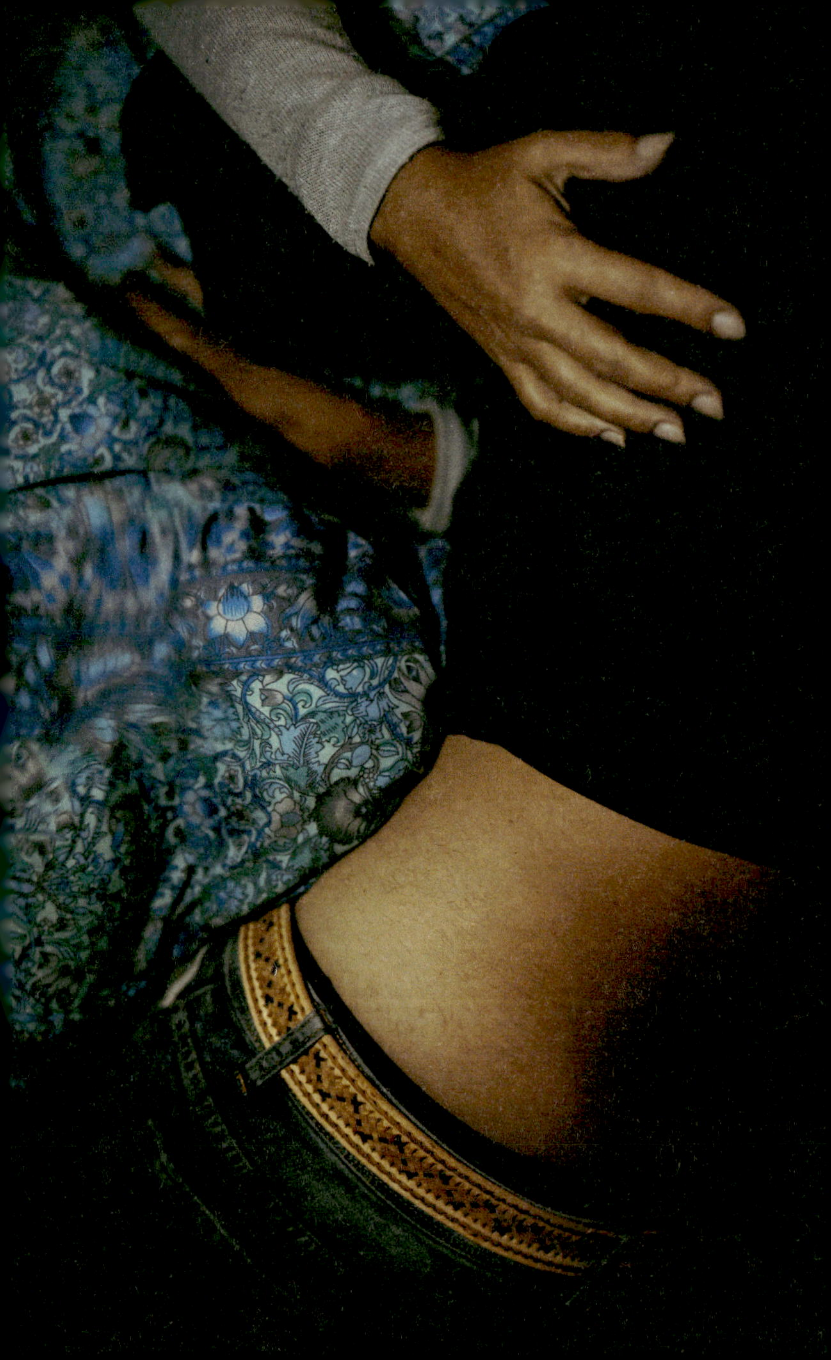

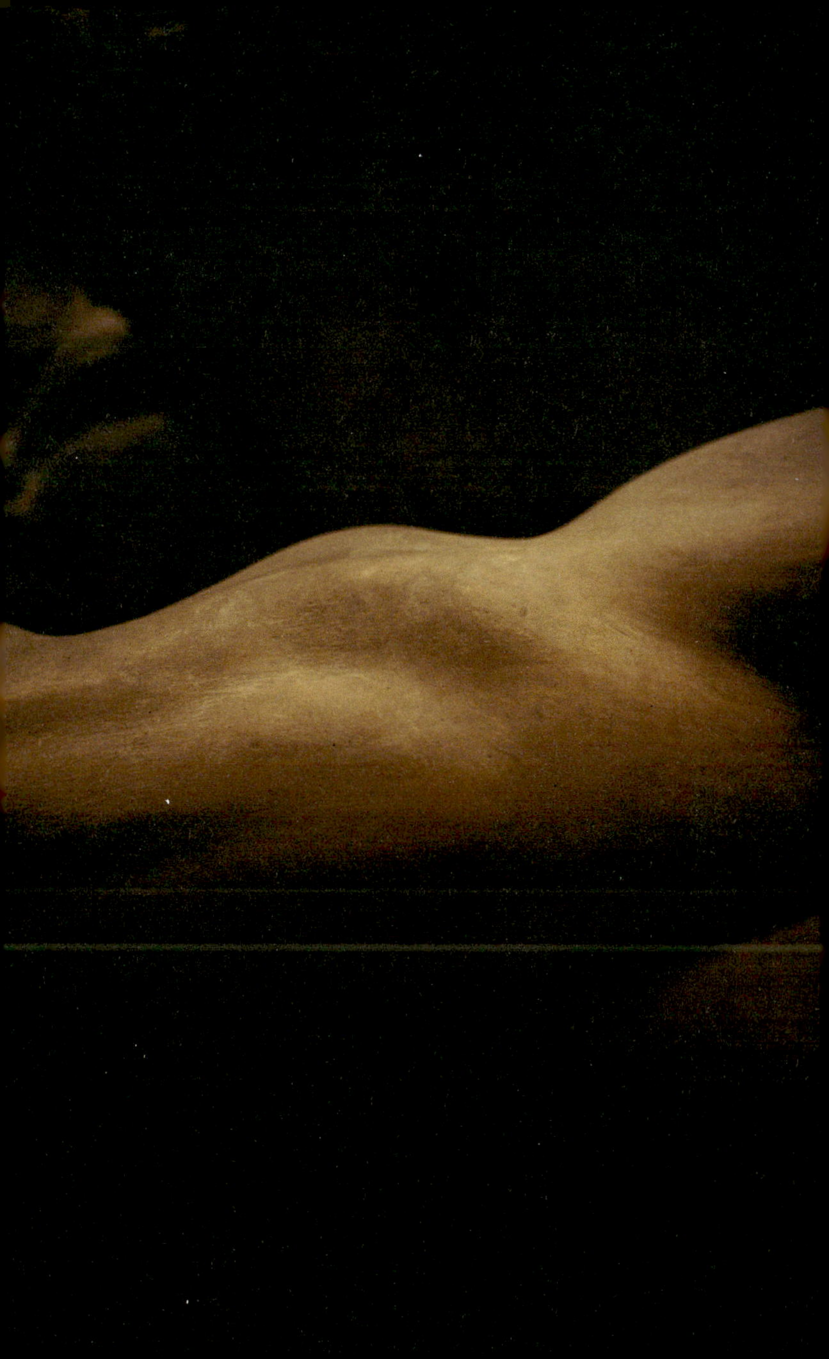

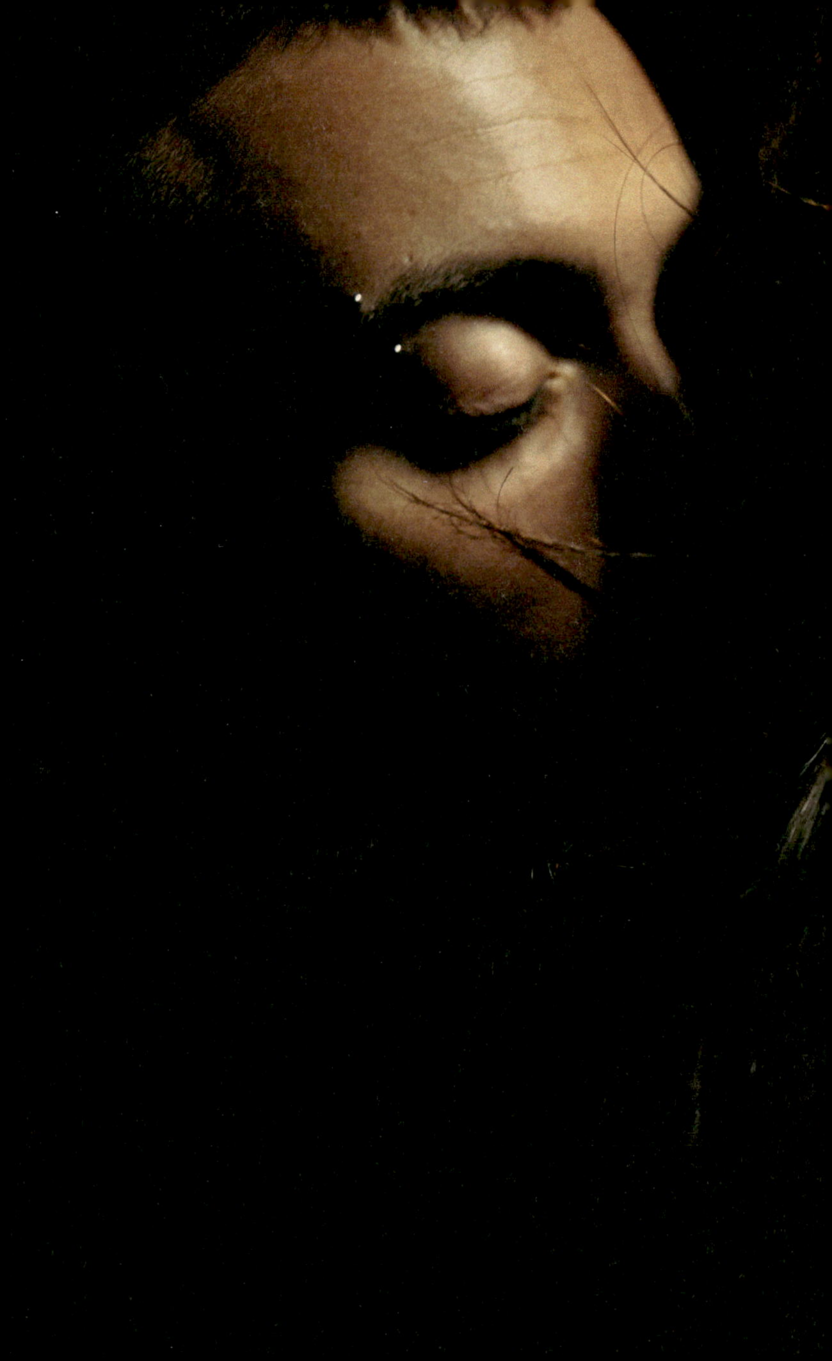

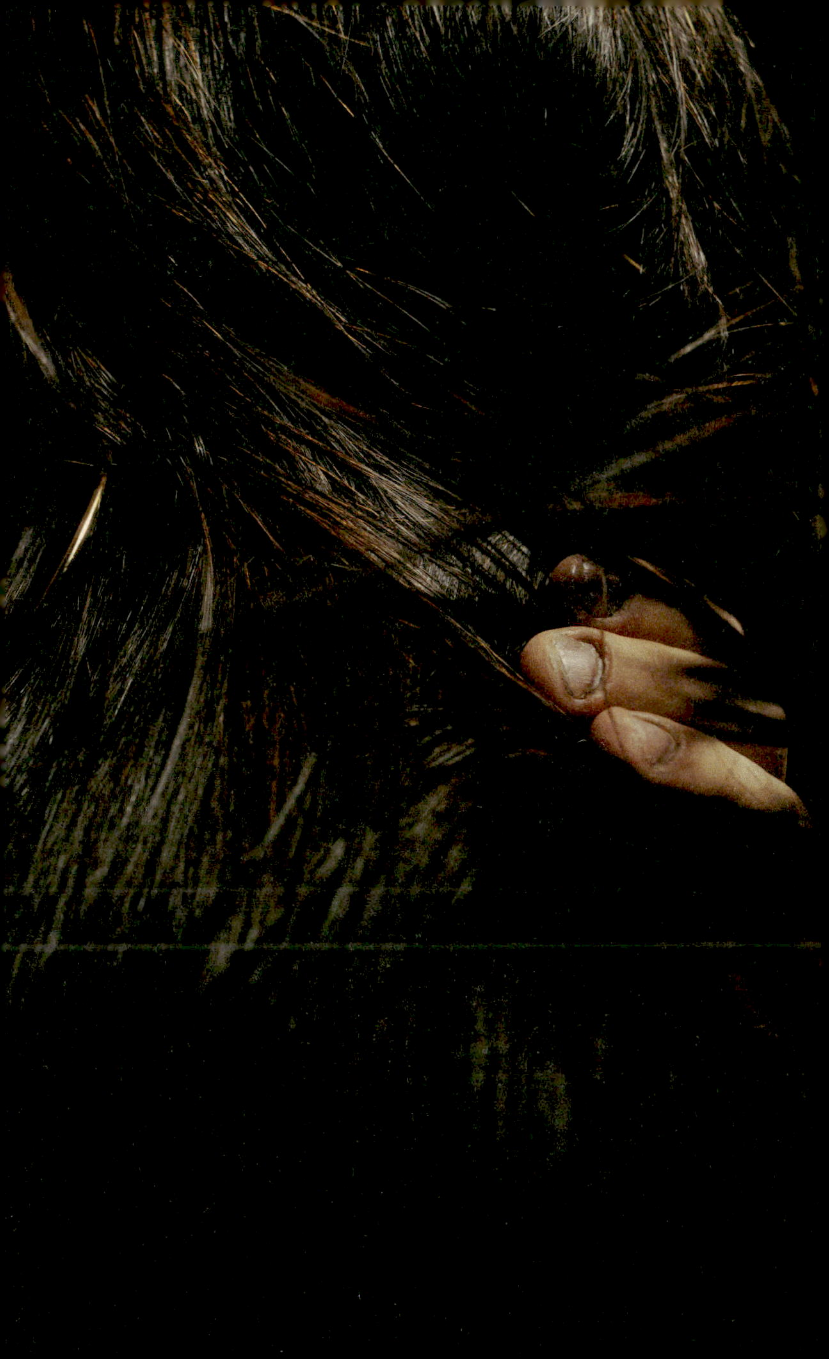

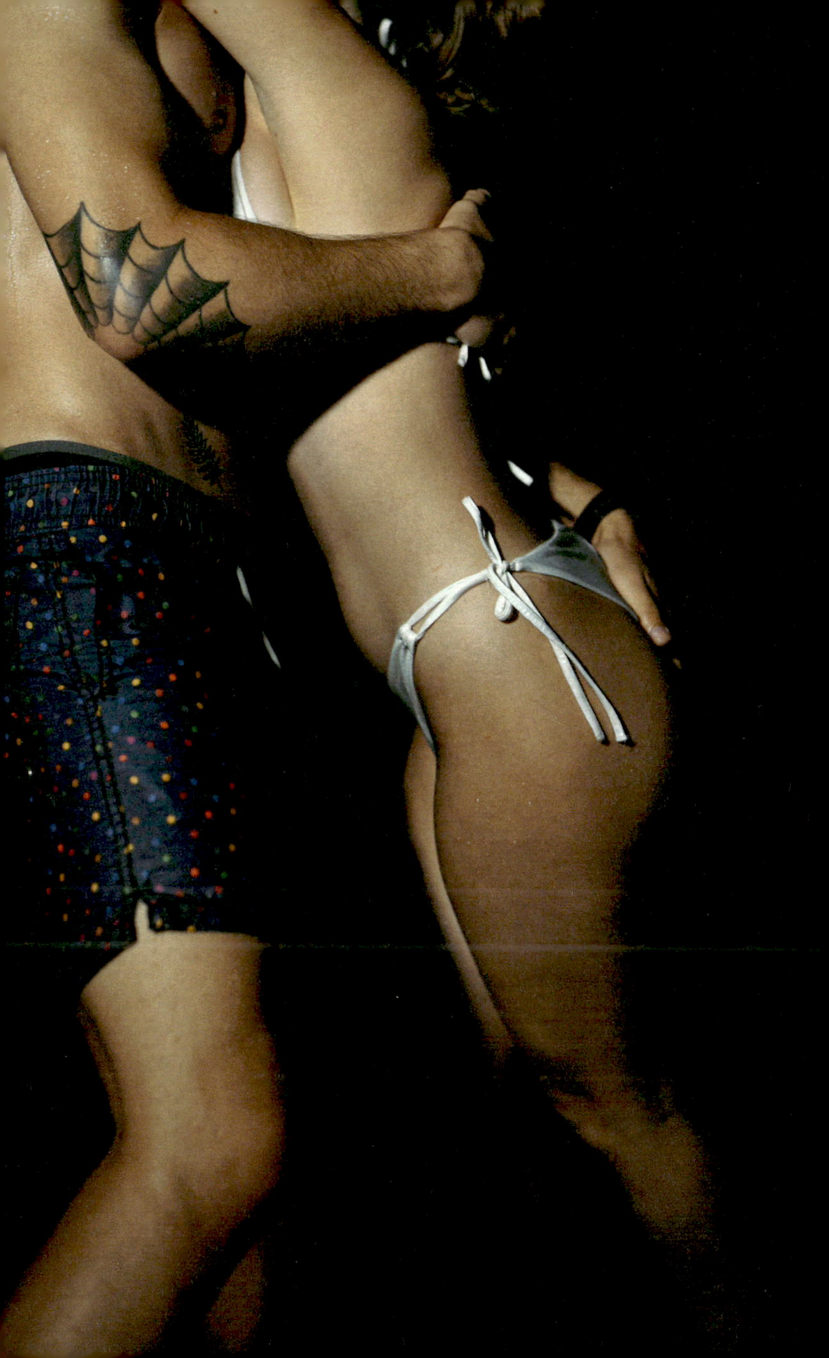

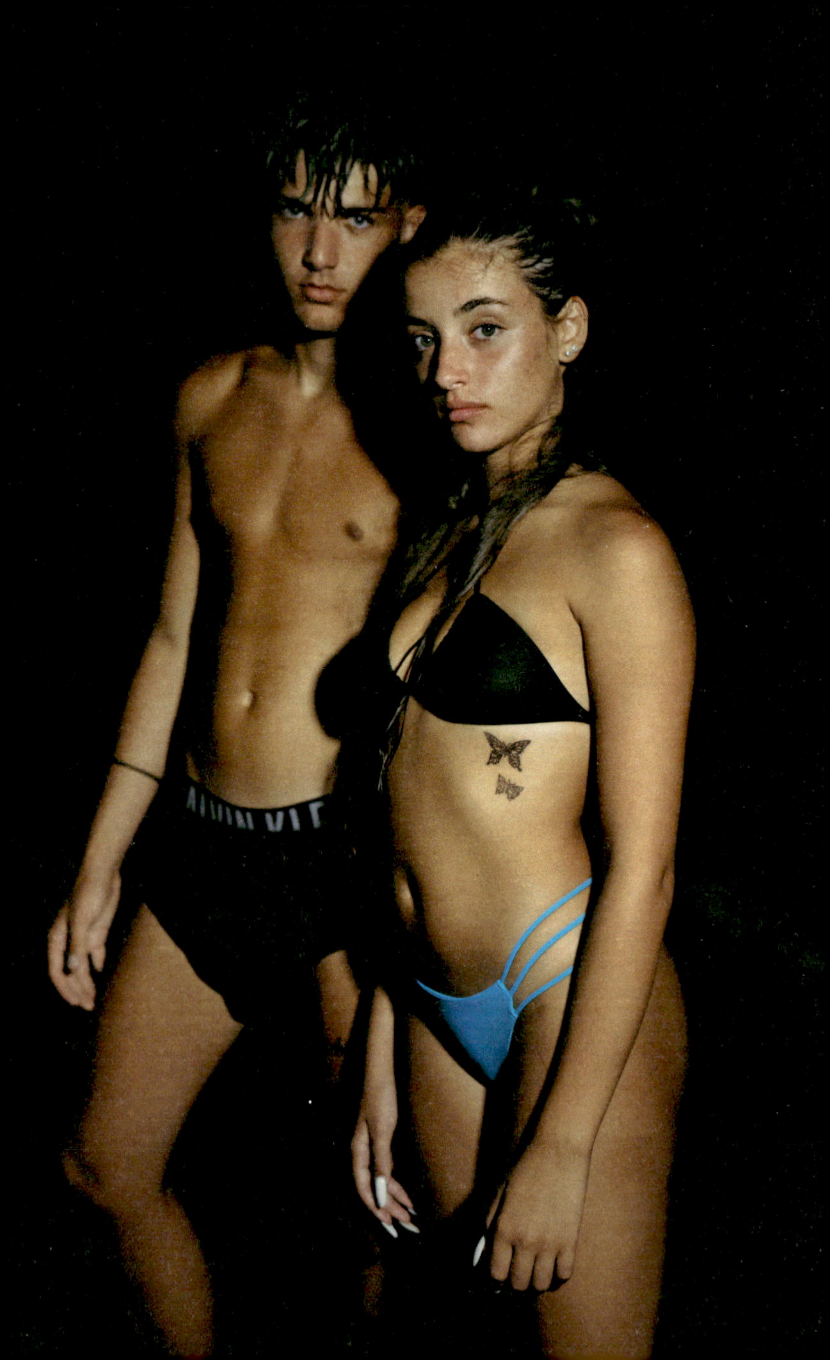

About Three Lives

ELENA MEDEL

A birthmark shaped like an apple or doughnut, depending on which craving your pregnant mother ignored. The scar from that fall when you took your first steps: while learning to fall, you cried a lot, more because you made a mistake than because it hurt. A word or a drawing – a bird, a heart – with which to fix in place the presence of a relationship, love or a friendship; even if it ends, even if it's forgotten, the tattoo awakens the memory. The incisions across your stomach from an operation. A ladleful of still-boiling soup you spilled on yourself while serving, leaving a wound which hardened after it became infected. Moles and marks that identify you and spare your loved ones the sight of your disfigured face after a car crash, of your flesh burned in a fire; not your destroyed body, but an isolated fragment of who you were. At the morgue they lift a sheet to show the mark on the shinbone you fractured, the name of someone no one will call and tell.

★

As soon as you think of the word *scar*, a line is drawn around your knee. You feel the pain of flesh splitting with the idea; on the way toward sound, the scab forms and the skin stretches. The scar retains its tightness despite the years gone by and the shine has yet to dull: after all, the scar – the idea, the symbol, the sign – celebrates that the damage has been repaired. At the morgue they'll lift a sheet to show the mark on the shinbone you fractured, the name of someone no one will call and tell: that's how they'll know it's you. At a bar you're talking to someone who doesn't need to ask what you do, because the answer is in the dry, cracked skin of your hands, the hardness of your palms. The body's language does its job. Maybe you've cut your nails short, but no matter how much soap and water you use, you can't suppress the dark lining surrounding the cuticles: the language of the body asserts itself. Its words seize control.

*

The body, using its language, also says other words. It says "effort" when, in a bar, you're talking to someone who doesn't need to ask what you do, because the answer is in the dry, cracked skin of your hands, the hardness of your palms. It says "company" the instant your arm subtly touches another on public transport: on the train or the bus, the fabric of your sweater rubbing against the bare skin of the person sitting next to you. The body may say "rejection" and move a centimeter away – touch, reaction, distance – or the body may say "desire." Even if nothing is happening: even if it's just an arm brushing against another arm on public transport, one body, another body, surrounded by others coming home from the office or escaping into the night, just for a moment; even if it's just an arm covered in the thin fabric of a cheap sweater next to an arm that's bare because they were running to try and make it on time. Even though nothing is happening, the body will say "desire," its mouth contracted and biting itself, its fists closed, its toes curling.

*

Or you missed the bus, the train: your exit from work was prolonged because you were asked to do something that wasn't part of your job at the last minute, or you were in your room getting ready and got distracted by a video on your phone. The body hides nothing. The birthmark in the shape of an apple or a doughnut, a bird tattooed on your chest – close to your heart – and a heart tattooed on the back of your hand – where it takes flight – or a badly healed wound. The blemish doesn't go away, it tells a story. The tattoo doesn't go away, it tells a story. The wound doesn't go away, it tells a story. These marks fade without muting the trace of the history that brought them to life. Now on the train or on the bus, one body, another body, surrounded by others coming home from the office or escaping into the night, just for a moment: the decision to stay put if something catches your interest, to move if it makes you uncomfortable. The body's language does its job. Too much heat. The naked arm brushing against the arm covered in cheap fabric belongs to you. Then, say "rejection" or say "desire."

⋆

Say "rejection," then, or say "desire." Say "mark" or "tattoo" or "scar," and think about the way its meaning was written on your body. Remember when you used to call it "skin," nothing more: the naked, most delicate tissue that acquiesces to scratches and drops of blood, that most delicate tissue which brushes against someone else's arm on public transport. Nothing more than hair and nerves and glands and fat and fat and fat and endless scientific names no one thinks about, although they exist. There was a time when the skin was bare, still without a story to tell. Then came the blemish or tattoo or scar, whose dense weight settled in your memory. It left a deep mark. After all those years, and all those bodies, it is still burnt into your memory, and the body doesn't hide it. Fine, soft hairs and moles run alongside various possible lives, distinct lives: there was a time of bare skin, there was a time of scarring, and then – forever – the time of scarred skin.

⋆

There was a time of bare skin.

There was a time of scarring. The hint of powerful ink before the laser, the false tone that replaces real skin.

Then there was the time when the skin was scarred.

We know there was also a period when time was suspended. Everything happened as it should: the sun comes up, you fill the hours, the sun goes down, and the cycle repeats.

Maybe you got up early and caught the bus or train to fulfill your duties. Maybe you were carrying boxes. You offered your arm, thin, cheap fabric: say "company" or "familiarity," or say "danger."

Maybe, between day and night, life happened, with the inertia of inwardly closing doors. Then you would recover your days.

There was a time of bare skin.

There was a time of scarring. So unexpected that you don't know how it inscribed itself on your body. Moles and contusions, marks and scars, a fresh wound or a thick layer of ointment covering the tattoo. The silence in the face of rejection. The silence in the face of desire.

Nothing that you learned was of any use now.

⋆

The sun came up. You filled the hours. The sun went down. Your habits repeated, one more time. Little by little, the life before the time of suspense. An arm that brushes another arm on public transport, one body, another body, surrounded by those coming home from the office or escaping into the night, just for a moment. Learning the path along which words travel. Thinking about the idea that is faithful to how much we want to express, choosing the word that travels from idea to sound, from idea to writing, say "mark" or "tattoo" or "scar." Which mark for this era, on the body, in the memory: with which animal or flower will you represent, on your ankle, the loneliness of not hearing other voices, not touching other bodies, saying goodbye to the people we loved. A jaguar representing life. A chrysanthemum for mourning. The six petals of the alstroemeria, as a symbol of friendship. The swan of idealized love. The route the scissors took near your elbow, so the pain wouldn't let you forget that you were still living, in spite of everything. The palm of another's hand pressing into your back in an embrace.

⋆

The sun came up. You filled the hours. The sun went down. New life, once again. You don't need birthmarks, tattoos, or scars to be identified by your loved ones, to spare them the sight of your disfigured face after an accident, of your flesh burned in a fire. Not yet. Now you have life and time; you have the body where you'll record the memory of your errors and all the future holds for you. On public transport, your arm will brush against someone else's: you'll say "desire." To someplace you will say "desire." Tonight you'll shout the words with the roar of a jaguar, you'll slip between the bodies with the promise of a swan. You'll flower like the alstroemeria and close like the chrysanthemum. The vivid weight of the hand on your back when they embrace you: the strength of your hand on the back of the body between yours. You'll say "desire." You'll also say: the pain that anchors us so that we'll stay. You'll say "desire."

⋆

Various possible lives, various distinct lives: there was a time of bare skin, there was a time of scarring that comes to pass – of the memory forged; that comes to pass – then there was forever the time of scarred skin. The body's language did its job. There was a path the words took, from idea to music, from idea to form: you said "company," you said "rejection," you said "desire." Your identity is in the words that become flesh, that take hold. Moles and marks. To know you, it's enough simply to feel your rough skin, which tells your story; to see symbols that point to memories – you'll say "mark" or you'll say "tattoo" or you'll say "scar." After animal nights comes day, breaking its habit. Again: after animal nights comes day, breaking its habit. How many lives? How many possible lives, how many distinct lives? Say "three lives." Say "about three." Say which.

I would like to thank all the people who made this book possible. My family for always being close to me. Gabriel Titire and Desiree Trentini for their company during the endless nights at Lido di Ostia. Juanjo Justicia, Lucía Peluffo and José Quintanilla for their generosity. Maarten Schilt and César Martínez-Useros for believing in this project. The Benicàssim Town Council for its collaboration. And especially Shirin Salehi for her profound gaze and unconditional support in the creation of this book.

Dedicated to the couples who loved each other on the beaches of Rome and to all the people who dared to live again.

Mar Sáez

The project *Terza Vita* was carried out with support from MAEC-AECID grants for Art, Education and Culture at the Academy of Spain in Rome.

ISBN 978 90 5330 960 5

Photography
Mar Sáez

Text
Elena Medel

Edit
Lucía Peluffo & Mar Sáez

Design
underbau, Madrid

Text correction
Darío García, New York
Tomas Brogan, Amsterdam

Prepress
La Troupe, Madrid

Printing & Binding
Artes Gráficas Palermo, Madrid

Schilt Publishing books are available worldwide at quality brick-and-mortar (art)bookstores, online stores, as well as at www.schiltpublishing.com

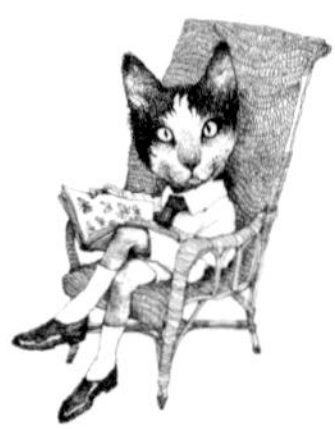